The Canadian Money Market
Revised

The Canadian Money Market
Revised

Wood Gundy Limited

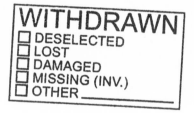

McGraw-Hill Ryerson Limited

Toronto Montreal New York London Sydney
Johannesburg Mexico Panama Düsseldorf
Singapore Sao Paulo Kuala Lumpur New Delhi

The Canadian Money Market, Revised

ISBN 0-07-092658-1

Library of Congress Catalog Card Number
73-15082

12345678910   D   3210987654

Printed and bound in Canada

Table of Contents

Appendices

Preface

This book provides a snapshot of the Canadian Money Market as it exists at the time of writing in early 1973. Originally published in 1956 under the title *Discount Paper in Canada,* this edition represents the third complete overhaul and revision of such material as is considered relevant to an understanding of the Canadian Money Market. The book is designed to serve two purposes. First, it is hoped that those who are not familiar with the Canadian Money Market will find the book useful as an introduction to the market. Second, for those who are already familiar with the market, it is thought that the book may serve as a useful reference source from a technical point of view.

A number of readers may be unfamiliar with the functions performed by Canadian Investment Dealers in general and Wood Gundy Limited in particular. Since the establishment of our Company in 1905, the organization has grown to become one of the largest investment dealers in Canada. With a staff of approximately 900 located in 20 cities across Canada as well as in New York, London and Tokyo, Wood Gundy Limited provides a complete investment service to governments, corporations, financial institutions, and individual investors. Our range of services includes the underwriting and distribution of government and corporate securities in principal financial markets; stock brokerage facilities on all major Canadian exchanges and on the New York Stock Exchange, the Midwest Stock Exchange, and the Philadelphia-Baltimore-Washington Exchange; over-the-counter trading of stocks and bonds; money management for individuals; pension fund measurement; payroll investment services; mortgage advisory services; investment research designed for financial institutions and the individual and corporate investor; over-the-counter markets in Eurobonds and Premium Dollar investment funds in London; as well as the services Wood Gundy Limited provides as a dealer and broker in the money and foreign exchange markets.

Wood Gundy Limited has an experienced staff of money market specialists located in offices in Toronto, Montreal, Vancouver, New York and London, England. In addition, experienced money specialists are continuously operating throughout other financial centers. In this book, we hope that we are able to convey from our experience the ingredients of what we regard as a fascinating, exacting and fun business to be in.

The information contained in this book is drawn from sources that we believe to be reliable; however, Wood Gundy Limited does not guarantee its accuracy or currency. Individual financial and legal advice should be obtained before action is taken in reliance on the information.

Peter Campbell

Vice-President and Director   *December, 1973*

Chapter I

The Canadian Money Market

The Nature and Function of a Money Market

A Money Market is a market where money, in the sense of an acceptable means of payment, is traded between those who have a short-term need for funds in excess of internally generated availability and those who have a supply of funds in excess of immediate requirements. The price structure generated by this market is a myriad of interest rates which is represented by the short-term spectrum of the term structure of interest rates. In practice, the bulk of money market transactions represents a term to maturity of less than one year. The market in Canada is divided into two broad areas, the Official Money Market and the Private Money Market.

The Official Money Market

The Official Money Market includes sixteen investment dealers authorized by the Bank of Canada. Authorization involves the granting of a credit facility by the Bank of Canada to the dealers, secured by "designated collateral" if the facility is activated. Designated collateral includes Government of Canada treasury bills, Government of Canada direct and guaranteed bonds having a term to maturity of less than three years, and Bankers' Acceptances up to a predetermined percentage of the dealer's credit facility. When a dealer activates his credit facility with the Bank of Canada, the transaction is called a "Purchase and Resale Agreement" (PRA). The Bank of Canada purchases securities from a dealer on the understanding that they will be resold to the dealer in the near future. When a dealer receives PRA accommodation from the Bank of Canada, the cost of the transaction (or the interest rate charged by the Bank of Canada) is the most recent 91-day Government of Canada treasury bill tender average plus ¼ of 1% —subject to a minimum level of Bank Rate less ¾ of 1% and a maximum of Bank Rate. The Bank Rate is the minimum rate at which the Bank of Canada will make advances to the Canadian chartered banks. A bank in Canada is chartered federally by the Bank Act, hence the use of the term "chartered bank." The reason for the PRA procedure is that the Bank of Canada is not empowered in law to lend to anyone other than the government sector and the Canadian banks.

The Canadian chartered banks will advance funds to the authorized money market dealers on an overnight basis subject to renegotiation or call prior to 12 h (noon) the following day. These funds are known as "Day Money" and the rate paid by the dealers is known as the "Day Rate." These Day Money Loans are secured by designated collateral provided that the total of the dealer's Day Money Loans plus Purchase and Resale Agreements outstanding does not exceed the dealer's credit facility with the Bank of Canada. The Day Money Market is used by the chartered banks to adjust cash reserves, and Day Money Loans form a part of the banks' statutory secondary reserve requirements. In contrast to the United States there is only one kind of money in Canada, clearing house funds; there is no continuously operational equivalent to U.S. Federal Funds.

The combination of the extension of Bank Credit facilities

to authorized dealers and the Day Money Loan Market serve to create active secondary markets in the designated collateral. Wood Gundy Limited is an authorized dealer and continuously makes competitive markets in designated collateral thus contributing in an important way to the depth, breadth and resiliency of the Official Money Market in Canada.

The Private Money Market

Virtually all Canadian provinces, major municipalities, institutions, and corporations participate in the Private Money Market either as borrowers or lenders. The principal vehicles are: promissory notes of provinces and municipalities; deposits and deposit receipts of banks and trust and mortgage loan companies; promissory notes of sales finance companies and of commercial and industrial corporations.

Certain investment dealers act both as dealers and money brokers in the Private Money Market. The Private Money Market activities of these firms are regulated by the Investment Dealers Association of Canada. Their money market staffs are licensed by the relevant Provincial Securities Commissions in Canada and by the relevant authorities in the United States.

The Size of the Canadian Money Market

Appendix A indicates the approximate size of the Canadian Money Market as at year end from 1969 to 1972 from a lender's point of view by asset category. At the end of 1972 the total market was in excess of $23 billion. The Official Market was about $10 billion with the balance being the Private Market.

In relative terms, restrictions on non-resident participation in the Canadian Money Market and Canadian participation in other Money Markets, are minor. Accordingly, the Canadian Money Market must be viewed as being part of the World Money Market. The World Money Market is huge in relation to the Canadian Money Market. The Canadian Market is, therefore, particularly sensitive to developments abroad and considerations of its size must always be placed in this broader context.

Chapter II

Portfolio Development

From a lender's point of view, there are five important factors in determining the nature of money market participation.

Cash is a Sin

From a balance sheet point of view, the object of financial administration is to maximize the return on assets and minimize the cost of liabilities. Cash does not generate a return. Thus the objective of cash flow management is to meet all current payments without running a significant cash balance at the close of business each day. The Money Market facilitates this objective.

Quality

Safety of principal is paramount. Standard procedure among lenders is for the appropriate line staff in the Treasury Area to collate credit worthiness information and make representations to their Board of Directors. The Board, in turn, accepts or rejects proposals for additions to what is known as the company's "approved list." Once names are approved, mandatory limits for each name are often inserted to both limit and spread risk. The approved list is then reapproved at appropriate intervals with additions and deletions. Such credit decisions are corporate decisions.

Return

The rate of interest that can be expected on any short-term investment depends primarily on the interest rate structure prevailing in the country at that time and the interest arbitrage opportunities among equivalent investments in other national financial markets. The return is also a function of the degree of credit risk undertaken, as well as the desired term and liquidity.

Liquidity

Liquidity refers to the speed and certainty with which an investment may be sold before maturity if the need arises. This marketability is an important factor in the yield to be obtained. If a high degree of liquidity is required at all times, then a commensurately lower yield can normally be expected. The use of borrower and dealer call features enhances liquidity.

Term

The yield curve is normally upward sloping indicating that very short dated yields are generally lower than longer dated yields. The reason for this is that lenders generally feel more liquid when holding a short dated security and borrowers feel more liquid when issuing a longer dated security. Accordingly, lenders are generally willing to accept a lower yield for short dates and borrowers are prepared to pay a premium for long dates. From a lender's point of view then, it is usually the case that the longer the term for which funds can be put out, the higher the yield. A term suitable to the lender can normally be arranged either directly or with the use of the "buy-back" or "repurchase" (repo) technique. The longer the term, the more an investor is exposed to market risk or to potential loss/gain should portfolio liquidation be required prior to maturity.

An Approach to Portfolio Management

Given the foregoing considerations, there would appear to be four elements in developing an appropriate portfolio strategy.

Near Cash

This section of a money market portfolio constitutes a cushion of highly liquid reserves to allow for daily operational needs as unexpected cash requirements arise. The percentage of the total portfolio or absolute amount to be invested in this manner depends on the standard variances in corporate cash flow from forecast. Care is essential to ensure that a desire for increased return does not decrease the size of the near cash cushion to the point where frequent sales of less liquid securities become necessary.

Specific Maturities

Certain cash requirements can be foreseen quite readily. These include: taxes, interest on funded debt, dividends, redemption of outstanding issues, sinking fund commitments, and progress payments on new construction. In this section of the money market portfolio, maturities can be synchronized to coincide with these outlays. Higher yields may be expected than in the near cash section since liquidity is not essential.

Contigencies

This reserve represents yet another form of surplus cash employment, but unlike the investments in the previous sections, these are of a more permanent nature. The uses that might arise for these funds include: inventory stockpiling, mergers or acquisitions, uninsured losses, plant expansion and other contingencies not quantifiable in the near term. The longer average term of the securities offsetting these contingencies, combined with a decreased need for liquidity, usually make this the highest yielding section of the portfolio.

Maturity Mix

In a market where there is no discernible direction to the movement in interest rates either a neutral or a "dumbbell" maturity mix is appropriate depending on the portfolio manager's tolerance for risk. A neutral maturity mix is one that has a fairly even maturity distribution out to the limit of the portfolio manager's time horizon. The dumbbell maturity mix is one that lumps maturities approximately equally between very short dated and very long dated investments in order to take advantage of generally higher yields in the longer dates but allows for flexibility when a trend in yield develops by spinning out the short dates if yields begin to fall and not extending term if yields begin to rise. In a market where yields are tending lower, an aggressive maturity mix would include a skewing of the portfolio in the direction of longer dates. Conversely, in a market where yields are tending higher, a skewing of the maturity mix in a defensive short dated direction is appropriate.

The foregoing approach to short-term portfolio development should result in the optimum use of surplus cash flow.

Chapter III

The Instruments

There is a wide range of continuously evolving instruments and techniques in the Canadian Money Market. The more important of these are examined in turn. Where applicable, Appendix A indicates the amounts outstanding of each.

Government of Canada Securities

Treasury Bills

The Bank of Canada, as agent for the Government of Canada, calls for tenders at noon each Thursday on a previously specified number of treasury bills. The normal terms at issue are for 91 days and 182 days, but occasionally terms of 270 days and 364 days are issued. If the latest 91-day bills are too long an investment, then suitable shorter bills from previous auctions can normally be offered by a dealer. A secondary trading market assures a high degree of liquidity.

Treasury bills are available in bearer form only and are sold at a discount to mature at par. Under the Income Tax Act the increment between the purchase price and the sale price or redemption value is treated as income. Treasury bills are available in denominations of $1,000, $5,000, $25,000, $100,000, and $1,000,000 and settlement may be arranged the same or the following day.

Repurchase Agreements or "Buy-Backs"

Repurchase agreements on Canada bills can be entered into between the purchaser and the dealer in the case where a particular maturity required is not available and liquidity is not essential. These agreements involve the purchase by the investor of treasury bills with a maturity longer than the date specifically required. At the same time, the investment dealer contracts to buy back or repurchase the bills prior to their maturity on the specific date that funds are required by the investor. The predetermined differential between purchase price and sale price provides the investor with a fixed return for the desired term.

Canada and Canada Guaranteed Bonds

Short-term federal government bonds are usually in good supply and, therefore, enjoy an active market with attendant advantages of liquidity. These securities are available in fully registered or registered as to principal only or bearer form. Settlement is normally concluded on the second business day following the transaction, but delivery can be arranged against payment on other dates.

Provincial Government Securities

Canadian provinces, either directly or through their various guaranteed authorities, make use of the Money Market for short-term financing on a continuing basis. Repayment of provincial and provincially guaranteed borrowings rests not only upon the general credit of the issuing government, but also upon its taxing power. Consequently, they are second only to federal government obligations in credit standing.

Types of Instruments

There are several types of provincial treasury bills or promissory notes. Some are sold at a discount; others bear a fixed rate of interest; a few combine both of these features.

Certain provinces issue notes on a "tap basis," tailored to meet the specific maturity required by the lender. Other provinces issue bills in a manner similar to Canada treasury bills. While issuing procedures differ, generally speaking $25,000 denominations are available in either bearer or registered form. Continuous borrowers on a tap basis include the Hydro Electric Power Commission of Ontario and Hydro Quebec. Continuous borrowers on a tender basis include Alberta, Manitoba, Ontario and Saskatchewan.

Outstanding Issues

As the term of outstanding provincial debentures originally issued as long-term debt approaches maturity, they tend to become part of the Money Market.

Liquidity

Investment dealers in the money market continuously provide competitive, secondary markets in provincial securities.

Municipal Government Securities

A number of major Canadian municipalities have found the Money Market a convenient source of temporary financing. Funds are raised to meet current expenditures prior to tax receipts, or to finance capital expenditures for which long-term debt will subsequently be issued. Municipal borrowings fall under the surveillance of the appropriate authority in each province. The restrictions as to purpose and amount vary from province to province.

Types of Instruments

Municipalities follow practices similar to the provinces in the issuance of promissory notes. Liquidity, however, may be more limited. While terms vary considerably, most are less than 90 days and can often be arranged to meet the lender's requirements. Denominations of $100,000 or more in either fully registered or bearer form are customary.

Taxation Note

Federal, provincial and municipal securities are free of withholding tax if purchased by non-residents. Appendix B contains a schedule of the incidence of Canadian withholding tax.

Canadian Chartered Bank Securities

Canadian banks have extensive branch networks throughout Canada and most have significant branch and agency business offshore. The following table indicates the size of the Canadian banking system.

ASSETS OF THE CANADIAN BANKING SYSTEM
AS AT MARCH 31, 1973

Bank	Assets (Millions of Dollars)
Bank of Montreal	12,294
The Bank of Nova Scotia	9,340
The Toronto-Dominion Bank	8,271
La Banque Provinciale du Canada	1,781
Canadian Imperial Bank of Commerce	14,050
The Royal Bank of Canada	15,821
Banque Canadienne Nationale	2,977
The Mercantile Bank of Canada	482
Bank of British Columbia	256
Unity Bank of Canada	48
Total	65,321

Reference: Order of Incorporation; from *Supplement to The Canada Gazette*, May 5, 1973. Reproduced by permission of Information Canada.

Following are the major bank instruments that relate to the Money Market.

Bearer Deposit Notes

Secured by the general credit of the issuing bank, bearer deposit notes are sold at a discount to mature at par. Terms from 7 days up to 1 year are normally available, and denominations are in minimum amounts of $100,000. Because of their nature, chartered bank bearer deposit notes are particularly suitable for portfolios seeking prime credit, liquidity and a relatively competitive rate of return.

Deposit Receipts, Term Notes, Certificates of Deposit

All of the above names are used by the various chartered banks to describe their obligations of 1 day to 6 years in term. These instruments are sold in a wide variety of forms, with marked differences in liquidity and means of interest payment. Generally the minimum denomination is $5,000. Rates often vary between banks and are quoted on request.

U.S. Dollar Deposits

Canadian banks accept U.S. Dollar deposits from both Canadian and United States sources. These deposits are booked with the Canadian Head Office and transferred to the U.S. agency of the bank.

United States investors, both corporate and institutional, have often found that fixed-term U.S. Dollar deposits with Canadian banks offer higher yields than equivalent U.S. credits.

When purchased by U.S. residents, these deposits are not subject to either the 15% Canadian Non-Resident Withholding Tax nor to the United States Interest Equalization Tax. When purchased by Canadian residents, the 15% U.S. Non-Resident Withholding Tax does not apply.

Bank Swapped Deposits

From time to time the chartered banks can offer the short-term investor holding Canadian Dollars very attractive rates on "swapped" deposits. Otherwise known as a "bank swap," this non-liquid instrument is essentially a United States

Dollar deposit with a foreign exchange swap attached indicating that the Canadian investor enjoys protection from any exchange rate fluctuations.

In theory, the investor with Canadian Dollars must first convert them into U.S. Dollars in order to create the deposit. In order to avoid exposure to exchange fluctuations during the life of the investment, arrangement would then have to be made simultaneously to convert the U.S. Dollar proceeds back to Canadian Dollars at the predetermined maturity date. This double conversion process is known as a "swap" and takes place on the day the deposit is entered into. The exchange rates at which these two simultaneous transactions would take place form an integral part of the all-in yield of the investment.

In actual practice, the chartered banks quote an all-in yield in Canadian Dollar terms which includes *both* the U.S. Dollar deposit rate *and* the yield effect of the swap. The prospective investor thereby avoids the step-by-step process described above. Quoted rates may vary widely, depending on both the term required and the chartered bank. Hence a thorough survey of available yields should be made prior to investing in these fully-hedged U.S. Dollar deposits. Wood Gundy Limited's foreign exchange department is in continuous contact with the major foreign exchange banks in North America. Accordingly it is possible for them to receive the most important swap deposit rates with one phone call. Often the best package includes a swap with one bank and a deposit with another arranged by the dealer.

A Note on Bank Deposit Rate Ceilings

Canada does not have a *de jure* structure of bank deposit rate ceilings analogous to Regulation Q of the U.S. Federal Reserve System. From time to time, however, market conditions have forced a form of rate agreement upon the banks with the approval of Canada's monetary authorities, the Bank of Canada and the Minister of Finance. At time of writing, a deposit rate ceiling is in force affecting those Canadian Dollar deposits of the major Canadian chartered banks which have a term to maturity not exceeding one year.

Bankers' Acceptances

In June 1962, Bankers' Acceptances first appeared in the Canadian Money Market. This money market instrument is essentially a commercial draft drawn by a borrower for payment on a specified date and accepted, or guaranteed, by his bank. The bank's acceptance is signified by counter-signatures on the draft. Once a draft of this type has been so countersigned, it becomes a Banker's Acceptance backed by the credit of the accepting bank. Acceptances are eligible for rediscount at the Bank of Canada, and as security for Day Money Loans with the chartered banks. As such they form an integral part of the Money Market and trade actively. Rates available on Bankers' Acceptances are usually competitive with other chartered bank securities of similar term.

Bankers' Acceptances are limited usually to a period not exceeding 90 days from the date of acceptance. Acceptances are created in the following denominations: $100,000; $200,000; $300,000; $500,000; $1,000,000; or any multiple thereof.

Bankers' Acceptances in Canada are more akin to accommodation paper when viewed through London or New York eyes and are not related to identifiable transactions in international trade.

Trust Company Securities

There are some 61 Canadian trust companies, having over 500 offices across the country, that compete actively for deposit funds.

As at December 31, 1972, their total assets under administration exceeded $36 billion with funds managed for estates, trusts and agencies comprising over $27 billion of this total. Company and guaranteed funds totalled over $8 billion.

The majority of trust companies are provincially incorporated. However, several of the larger companies are federally incorporated and licensed under the Trust Companies Act. In either case, trust companies, due to the restrictive nature of the provisions under which they are governed, enjoy a prime credit rating.

The nature and liquidity of their investment portfolios are regulated by law, with their obligations not exceeding 12½ to 20 times capital and surplus depending upon jurisdiction of incorporation.

Trust Company Deposits

Because of the great diversity in nature of business and laws of incorporation, it is difficult to summarize precisely the characteristics of trust company securities. However, the obligations issued by these organizations are normally Trustee Investments for trustees under the same incorporating jurisdiction.

One Year and Under

The short-term instruments issued by trust companies vary in term from 24-hour demand up to 1 year. These investments are known by many different names including Deposit Receipts, Short-Term Guaranteed Trust Certificates, Guaranteed Investment Certificates and Guaranteed Investment Receipts. Comparative rates are available upon request and normally lie between yields on chartered bank instruments and prime finance company paper. They are issued in interest bearing, fully registered form with a minimum investment of $5,000.

Fixed-term trust company instruments are illiquid since they are neither redeemable nor transferable. However, the issuing trust company may sometimes waive these restrictions after negotiation with the holder or his agent.

One Year and Over

Issued for terms of up to 5 years and having a variety of names, these fixed-term securities offer rates that are normally more attractive than chartered bank deposits for equivalent periods of time. Available in interest bearing form and minimum denominations of $500, these term certificates are available only in fully registered form. Their liquidity can vary widely and, if required, is best negotiated in the form of prior redemption rights.

Mortgage Loan Company Securities

Total assets of mortgage loan companies were $4.8 billion as at December 31, 1972. Although usually smaller in size than the trust companies, and incorporated under different legislation, the mortgage loan companies issue securities having many characteristics in common with those of the trust companies. The rates on these securities are somewhat higher than the trust company rates.

Finance Company Securities

Canadian finance companies raise a substantial percentage of their cash requirements through short-term borrowings. The proceeds are generally used for financing a broad range of consumer durable goods at both the wholesale and retail levels. A recent trend has been for finance companies to de-emphasize auto financing and to concentrate on first and second mortgages and leasing. In addition, a growing number of large Canadian manufacturing and merchandising corporations have formed their own sales finance subsidiaries. The nature of incorporation, form of capitalization, and type of business vary widely among the different finance companies. Their short-term promissory notes may, therefore, be secured, unsecured and/or guaranteed by a parent corporation. Wood Gundy Limited has consolidated relevant information on major finance company borrowers in the Canadian Money Market into a loose leaf book. This book is kept updated quarterly and is available upon request by their clients. Appendix C contains a sample report.

Most finance companies file Canadian Sales Finance Long Form Reports (CANSAF) and Robert Morris Reports which ensure a high degree of financial disclosure for the public and for credit analysts. The short-term notes of the majority of these companies are generally authorized investments for life insurance, trust companies and pension funds.

Rates are changed from time to time by the various companies depending upon the total demand for and supply of short-term funds in the market and the companies' individual requirements within this market. Investment for terms ranging from a few days to several years may be arranged. The notes, which can be interest bearing or discount and fully registered or bearer, are issued in amounts as low as $5,000 but denominations of $25,000 or $50,000 are much more common. Certain companies have limitations as to the maximum amount of notes which may be outstanding at any one time.

A partial list of those finance companies for whom Wood Gundy Limited acts is contained in Appendix I.

Commercial Paper

Commercial paper is the name given to the unsecured promissory notes issued by a wide range of Canadian corporations. The market for commercial paper used to be restricted to larger, well-known companies, but this is changing and an increasing number of smaller credit-worthy corporations are now issuing commercial paper. The notes are backed by the general credit of the issuing corporation and are usually unsecured. In addition, unused bank lines of credit and/or a parental guarantee support most borrowers. In most cases, they are authorized investments for life insurance, trust companies, and pension funds.

Notes are usually issued in multiples of $1,000, subject to a minimum of $50,000, although a number of companies have minimums of $100,000. Maturities range from overnight to 1 year. The notes may be interest bearing or discount, fully registered or in bearer form. Wood Gundy Limited has consolidated relevant information on major commercial paper borrowers in the Canadian Money Market into a loose leaf book as noted earlier and it is available to their clients on request.

Notes are sometimes issued with a call feature. Under this arrangement the lender has the right, throughout the term of the note, to demand prepayment upon giving the borrower 24 hours' notice. Interest is computed on the basis of rates determined at the time the investment is made. The lender normally receives a higher rate of interest if the note runs to maturity than if payment is demanded earlier. From time to time, dealers place their call features on notes to assist the investment objectives of clients. Appendix I includes a partial list of those commercial paper borrowers for whom Wood Gundy Limited acts.

Call Loans to Investment Dealers

Short-term loans to investment dealers by banks, corporations and institutions form an integral part of the Canadian Money Market. From the dealer's point of view, loans are a means of financing inventory. Appendix D contains a recent balance sheet for Wood Gundy Limited. A significant portion of the liability side reflects the call loan market. From an investor's point of view, call loans provide a prime quality investment for temporarily surplus funds. The same-day call feature provides complete liquidity with no market risk.

Call loans are subject to call or rate negotiations up to 12 h (noon) each day, or later if prearranged. All types of money market instruments may be "collateralized" against call loans subject to the lender's requirements: Bankers' Acceptances, bank bearer deposit notes, provincial and municipal paper, commercial and finance paper, government bonds, as well as Canada treasury bills which have not been banked as Day Money Loans.

The call loan rate assumes a two-tiered structure. Designated Day Money Loan collateral banked outside the banking system approximates the Day Money Loan rate. Against other collateral, the rate ranges upwards averaging 1% to 2% above the Day Rate, depending on market conditions. The call loan rate bears an interdependent relationship with yields in the 30-day paper market.

Funds are usually accepted in multiples of $100,000. The lender has the right to refuse any particular collateral suggested. However, the interest paid on a call loan varies as to collateral the lender prefers.

Payment, and collateral safekeeping arrangements, may be made to suit a lender's particular requirements. Wood Gundy Limited will hold the collateral in vault safekeeping on the client's behalf. In this event, an underlying Collateral Loan Safekeeping Agreement is entered into, specifying the terms and conditions of these loans. A typical agreement is contained in Appendix E.

In all cases, letters confirm the origin, adjustment, or termination of any particular loan as arranged by telephone. Since change of ownership does not actually take place, contracts are not normally either drawn up or sent out.

Investment dealers maintain an agreed margin consistent with the Regulations of the Investment Dealers Association of Canada. Appendix F contains such margin regulations. Since normal daily business may involve the selling of some of the securities offered as collateral, a dealer needs to retain the power of substitution.

Reverse Loans

From time to time an investor may need cash to meet a very short run requirement but not wish to liquidate certain money market investments. A common procedure for meeting this situation is known as a "reverse loan." The investor will sell to a dealer sufficient securities on a call basis to meet the requirement. The cost to the investor for his accommodation is call loan rate plus a spread for servicing the transaction. This cost is generally lower than alternative sources of funds.

Payment and Delivery

The great majority of payments and deliveries for money market securities are transacted through the facilities of chartered banks, trust companies and investment dealers in major centres.

Settlement

Settlement is normally made on the same day as the transaction is agreed upon. On occasion, however, transactions can be negotiated some time ahead of the actual settlement date.

Payment may be made directly by the lender upon receipt of the instrument in proper form, or alternatively an agent may be authorized to pay out funds against proper delivery. In practice, most lenders and borrowers accept Wood Gundy Limited's written undertaking to deliver securities at a later time. This facilitates the flow of funds and adds to the flexibility of the market place. Payment can also be made to any one of our offices in Canada, New York or London avoiding the cost of wire transfers. A large number of our clients avail themselves of the safekeeping service which we provide.

Redemption

At maturity, the borrower makes the proceeds available to the lender under prearranged terms and conditions. The certified pay-off cheque may be made payable to the lender or, at times, to his authorized agent, and is made available against receipt of the maturing note.

In general, care must be taken at the outset of the transaction to ensure that all details of payment and delivery meet the requirements of all parties involved.

Money Market Arithmetic

Interest calculations in the Money Market are simple and straightforward. Appendix G illustrates the more common transactions and yield calculations.

The Stucture of Money Market Yields

A combination of relative net demand for funds, liquidity, and credit-worthiness determines the tiering of interest rates in the Canadian Money Market. The following list attempts to summarize normal tiering from low to high.

> Day Money Loans from the chartered banks
> Day Money Loans from non-banks
> Government of Canada obligations
> Bank Rate of the Bank of Canada
> Provincial securities
> Bankers' Acceptances
> Bank deposits

Municipal securities
Call loans to investment dealers from non-banks
Trust company deposits
Prime finance company paper
Prime commercial paper
Prime loan rate to commercial customers by the
    chartered banks

In periods of monetary restraint, the structure from Provincial securities through to prime commercial paper tends to drift up towards and occasionally through prime loan rate when the banking system is rationing credit. Conversely, in periods of monetary ease, the entire structure from prime commercial paper on up to Day Money Loans from non-banks tends to press in against Day Rate.

Chapter IV

International Participation

The Canadian economy is an open economy. From a financial point of view, this necessitates extensive channels of integration between the Canadian financial sector and those offshore. Those factors which have major relevance to the Canadian Money Market are examined in turn.

The Canadian Foreign Exchange Market

The foreign exchange market for the Canadian Dollar is a three-tiered affair. The first tier is the intra-bank market and is inclusive to the branch banking system in Canada. A trader for Bank A merely crosses, say, a Halifax importer's requirements with a Vancouver exporter's requirements, both clients of Bank A, and lifts out a turn. The second tier is known as the inter-bank market. This market is composed of the Canadian chartered banks active in foreign exchange, the Federal Government's Exchange Fund Account and a salaried broker of the Canadian Bankers' Association. When Bank A, for example, has an overage of U.S. Dollars during a day, he will inform the salaried broker of his intent to sell U.S. at price x. The broker then canvasses the other participants in this market and if, say, Bank B has an offsetting overage of Canadian Dollars, the parties are brought together at a mutually satisfactory price. It is often the case, however, that the entire inter-bank market is going in the same direction and lay-offs have to be sought elsewhere. This is the third tier, the international market. If overages cannot be laid off in the inter-bank market, the bank trader attempts to lay off in New York or elsewhere either directly with a U.S. foreign exchange bank or through his own U.S. agency who may choose to use the services of a foreign exchange broker. The New York market, in turn, is wired into the Continental markets centered in London. The three tiers operate simultaneously.

The location of a market is where you find it. Wood Gundy Limited's Canadian Dollar foreign exchange business is about evenly divided between Canada and the United States. In Canada the centres are Montreal, Toronto and Vancouver. In the United States, New York is the largest market but a reasonable percentage of activity is represented by foreign exchange banks in Boston, Chicago, Detroit, Los Angeles, San Francisco and Seattle.

Regular settlement in foreign exchange, usually same day, is known as a "spot" transaction. A transaction for settlement at a date in the future is known as a "forward" transaction. A simultaneous purchase of one currency spot and its sale forward is known as a "swap" transaction. In interest arbitraging, the word "hedge" tends to be interchangeable with "swap." The spot market has a depth in the tens of millions on a continuous basis at current prices. The depth of the forward market tails off to generally negotiated amounts and prices over one year. Swap quotes have similar depth depending on term.

Non-Resident Short-Term Investment in Canada

The economic development of Canada has been closely tied to investments by non-residents. In particular, the close proximity of the United States and Canadian financial markets has led to a substantial flow of short-term funds between the United States and Canada. Due to Canada's present exemption from the American Government's balance of payments guidelines, investment in Canadian short-term financial assets by United States institutions and corporations has remained interest-rate sensitive. Appendix H documents the source of this exemption and subsequent developments.

Investment by United States Residents in Instruments Denominated in Canadian Dollars

Canadian money market instruments with an initial term of no longer than nine months are available to U.S. residents. In certain instances, it is possible to arrange an investment for a term longer than nine months on a private placement basis, with the U.S. investor signing an "investment letter" in order that the investment be exempt from the registration provisions of the Securities Act of 1933.

Hedging

A U.S. Dollar investor purchasing an instrument denominated in Canadian funds can eliminate the risk of the Canadian Dollar being worth less on the maturity of the investment by hedging the funds.

The hedge of the funds consists of the purchase of the Canadian Dollars required to pay for the instrument and the simultaneous sale of the Canadian Dollars to be received on the maturity of the instrument. The hedge of the funds can be done with major United States, Canadian or European banks and can be written in the name of the investor or in the name of the dealer.

The net return to the U.S. Dollar investor may be higher or lower than the base Canadian rate depending upon whether the forward Canadian Dollar is sold at a price higher or lower than that paid for the Canadian Dollars. In any event, the hedge contract is settled on the terms agreed upon, regardless of the value of the Canadian Dollar on the maturity date of the instrument. Section 5 of Appendix G illustrates a typical hedged transaction.

U.S. Dollar Denominated Canadian Securities

Certain prime Canadian borrowers are willing to issue short-term debt which is denominated in foreign currencies, most often in U.S. Dollars. This may be done because of an underlying requirement for the foreign currency. Alternatively, the rationale may be a desire to facilitate investment by the non-resident purchaser, who thereby no longer needs to hedge the available funds.

A United States investor is quoted an all-in yield, usually on a 360-day basis which can be readily compared to alternative investments.

The borrower normally performs the hedge transaction. However, if exchange conditions suggest otherwise, or if a U.S. Dollar cash flow is anticipated, the proceeds may be converted to Canadian Dollars on a spot basis.

The Canadian Withholding Tax and Non-Resident Purchase of Canadian Money Market Instruments

Interest and discount income accruing to a non-resident from the purchase of a Canadian debt instrument may be subject to the Canadian Withholding Tax (Non-Resident Tax). Short-term obligations issued or guaranteed by any federal, provincial or municipal government are free from the withholding tax whereas most other short-term obligations currently are subject to a 15% tax.

In addition, non-resident purchasers of Canadian debt instruments should bear in mind the following considerations.

Interest Bearing and Discount Instruments

The withholding tax is to be deducted and withheld by the payer of the interest at the time the interest or discount amount is paid or credited to the non-resident.

In the case of discount obligations when a non-resident sells to a Canadian resident an obligation which had been issued in Canada, the excess of the proceeds received by the non-resident over *the issue price* of the obligation is deemed an interest payment except in the case of specifically excluded obligations. If the tax withheld is excessive, as would be the case if the non-resident has not held the obligation continuously since the date of issue, the non-resident must submit a claim for the return of the excess tax withheld.

Alternatively, if the obligation is sold by a Canadian resident to a non-resident and either at that time or a subsequent time the non-resident re-sells the obligation to the same Canadian resident, the withholding tax need only be based on the excess of the proceeds to the non-resident on the resale over the *price* of the obligation at the time of initial sale by the Canadian resident to the non-resident.

Hedged Transactions

In the case of a non-resident's purchase of a package consisting of:

1) a Canadian-pay instrument

2) a hedge contract

the withholding tax applies only to the income earned from the instrument.

Instruments Exempt from the Withholding Tax

Interest payable to a non-resident on the following is exempt from the withholding tax.

1) bonds, debentures, notes, mortgages, hypothecs or similar obligations issued after April 15, 1966 and before 1976:

a) of or guaranteed by the Government of Canada,

b) of the government of a province or an agent thereof,

c) of a municipality in Canada or a municipal or public body performing a function of government in Canada.

2) a deposit of a chartered bank denominated in other than Canadian funds.

Non-Resident Organizations Exempt from the Withholding Tax

1) Non-resident organizations that have qualified under Article X of the Canada-United States Reciprocal Tax convention may be granted an exemption from the withholding tax by the Canadian Government. Essentially these are religious, scientific, literary, educational, and charitable organizations.

2) A non-resident organization that establishes to the satisfaction of the Canadian Government that, among other things:

a) an income tax is imposed under the laws of the country of which it is resident,

b) the organization is not subject to the income tax of that country, and

c) the organization would be exempt from Canadian income tax if it were a resident of Canada or it was a trust or corporation established to administer an employees' superannuation fund or plan.

may obtain a certificate of exemption from the Canadian Government exempting it from withholding tax on interest on bonds, debentures, or similar obligations issued after June 13, 1963.

3) Non-resident insurance companies and fraternal benefit societies registered to carry on business in Canada under the Canadian and British Insurance Companies Act or under the Foreign Insurance Companies Act are exempt from the withholding tax.

The Canadian Witholding Tax as a Foreign Tax Credit

The Canadian Withholding Tax qualifies as an income tax and as such, subject to the limitations of Section 904 of the Internal Revenue Code, may be used as a credit against United States Income Tax under the Internal Revenue Code of 1954, as amended.

Canadian Short-Term Investment Abroad

On occasion, it is advantageous for a Canadian resident to purchase a short-term financial asset denominated in U.S. Dollars. For example, the rate of return on a U.S.-pay instrument hedged to Canadian Dollars may be more attractive than the return available from an equivalent domestic credit.

The following instruments denominated in U.S. Dollars are available.

a) *U.S.-pay deposit receipts of the Canadian banks*

These deposits offer prime credit, attractive rates, occasional prearranged liquidity and exemption from the United States Non-Resident Withholding Tax. When hedged to Canadian Dollars, they are referred to as 'swap deposits'. Deposit arrangements may be made directly with the banks in Canada or with their respective New York agencies or through a dealer.

b) *United States money market instruments*

These comprise instruments such as treasury bills, bankers' acceptances, negotiable certificates of deposit and industrial and finance company paper.

Interest income earned from U.S. sources by a non-resident of the U.S. is subject to the 30% U.S. Non-Resident Withholding Tax which, under the existing Foreign Tax Treaty between Canada and the United States, is reduced to 15%. However, original issue discount on non-interest-bearing obligations issued after March 31, 1972 and payable not more than 6 months from date of original issue is not subject to the U.S. Non-Resident Withholding Tax. Subject to the limitations of Section 126 of the Canadian Income Tax Act, United States withholding tax may be applied as a credit against Canadian income tax on U.S. source income.

c) *Eurodollar investments*

Negotiable London certificates of deposit and Eurodollar deposits frequently offer attractive investment mediums for investors subject to the limitations of the Canadian guidelines affecting investments in third countries (i.e. non U.S. and Canada). In order for Canada to retain unrestricted access to the U.S. capital market, Canada has formulated a set of guidelines to prevent "pass-through." In concept, Canada is not to be used as a jitney for funds passing from the U.S. to the rest of the world. At time of writing, Canadian governments and their instrumentalities are exempt from the Canadian guidelines. Individuals are similarly exempt except in the case of securities subject to the U.S. Interest Equalization Tax if purchased by U.S. residents. Corporations and non-financial companies have a basic $2.0 million exemption per annum, cumulative. Otherwise, third country investments must normally be matched by third country sourced funds.

A Canadian resident may generate U.S. Dollars through the sale of securities, the sale of assets or in the normal course of business. The funds may be required to meet future U.S. Dollar commitments and consideration should be given to investing them in instruments denominated in U.S. Dollars or in hedged Canadian-pay instruments.

Regardless of whether the Canadian investor starts with Canadian or U.S. Dollars, the decision to invest in an instrument denominated in U.S. Dollars depends upon tax considerations and the interest rate differential after appropriate hedging of funds.

The Eurocurrency Market

The Eurocurrency market is an international money market based upon deposits in Dollars and other convertible currencies. Eurodollars are U.S. Dollar deposits owned by non-residents of the United States, and in the same way, Deutschemarks on deposit in Zurich or Paris are known as Euromarks. Thus any convertible currency owned by a non-resident of the host country is referred to as a Eurocurrency. The prefix "Euro" may be a slight misnomer in that such deposits are not necessarily in Europe—they could be in Canada or Japan, for example, and still technically be part of the Eurocurrency market—but when the market began in the early 1950s with the shifting of Dollar deposits from New York to London, it was largely confined to Europe. Now it has trading centres throughout the world, in places such as Hong Kong, Singapore, Tokyo, Toronto and Nassau, as well as Europe, although London remains the leading location. The size of the Eurocurrency pool has grown enormously in recent years, from about $9 billion at the end of 1964 to about $100 billion at the end of 1972, with the Dollar share shrinking somewhat from about 80% to around 65% in the respective years.

Two essential characteristics of the Euromoney market are its freedom from the direct control of any national authority and its specialization in wholesale transactions. Although many countries regulate their residents' activities in the market and the Bank for International Settlements and certain central banks have occasionally conducted quasi-open-market operations, there are relatively few controls on banks' operations such as reserve ratios, special deposits or interest rate limitations. This means that interest rates are determined largely by the free interplay of demand and supply, although U.S. domestic short-term rates tend to be a floor to Eurodollar rates. The reason domestic U.S. rates tend to form a floor to the Euromarkets is that U.S. residents are restricted by the U.S. balance of payments programme in their dealings in Eurodollars while non-residents of the U.S. are not similarly restricted in their dealings in the U.S. Accordingly, when pressures force Euro-rates higher than domestic U.S., Americans cannot easily sell in the U.S. and buy in Europe whereas, when Euro-rates fall below U.S., then Europeans can sell in Europe and buy in the U.S. to take advantage of more attractive yields.

The wholesale nature of Eurocurrency transactions is reflected in the low spread at which banks are willing to deal. In contrast to national banking systems, the Eurocurrency market does not rely on expensive retail deposit-gathering where funds come in relatively small lots. Its deposits are placed almost exclusively by corporations, governments and wealthy individuals in minimum amounts of roughly $100,000 ranging up to many millions of Dollars.

Much of the activity in the market consists of simple, inter-bank transactions, with deposits initially placed by non-bank holders going through a series of lending and re-depositing operations at spreads as narrow as 1/32 of 1% and in minimum amounts of $500,000. Much of it is more complex, however, because the market is an important link-ing mechanism between national Money Markets. It has added very greatly to the degree of monetary integration among national systems through its capacity to mobilize short-term capital flows. The market has become the main channel for interest arbitrage, a vehicle for expressing views on currency values, and a source of funds for a broad range of multinational corporations. As a result, it is closely allied to foreign exchange markets, and banks shift sizable amounts very quickly from one market to another, taking advantage of interest rate differentials by swapping from one currency to another. The forward market mechanism in most currencies is, accordingly, extremely sensitive to changes in Eurodollar rates and will quickly be adjusted if out of line.

Borrowing in the Eurocurrency Market

The narrow spreads and large capacity of the Eurocurrency market make it an attractive source of funds for borrowers. Very large amounts up to several hundred million Dollars are raised quickly and cheaply by credit-worthy borrowers from every part of the globe, including borrowers from countries with extremely small and under-developed money markets.

Corporations and governments who are borrowing in the

Eurocurrency market normally do so under one of three methods, a line of credit, a revolving commitment or a specific situation loan. The line of credit pre-establishes the maximum amount which a bank is willing to lend, based on its credit examinations, in either Dollars or other convertible currencies. The funds are then extended as required but subject to availability on the part of the bank. A revolving commitment is similar except that it is normally established for a medium-term period and the funds are assured through a commitment fee charged on any unused portion of the loan. The specific situation loan is more likely to be used in the event that funds are required only for a short non-continuing period.

Rates on Eurocurrency loans may be fixed or floating, although loans of one year and under are normally fixed at London Inter-Bank Offering Rate (LIBOR) for the relevant term plus a spread depending on credit. Medium-term commitments quite often carry a rate that is altered every three or six months to reflect any change in LIBOR.

Investing in the Eurocurrency Market

Subject to complying with exchange control and balance of payments guideline restrictions, corporate and institutional investors can often invest at higher rates in the Eurodollar Money Market than in domestic markets.

Call and fixed-term Eurodeposits are available in Dollars, Marks, Swiss Francs, French Francs, Sterling, Guilders, Canadian Dollars and any other freely convertible currency in which there is a good forward exchange market, but normally there is no significant hedged interest rate advantage between these various Eurocurrency deposit rates due to arbitrage.

Non-Negotiable Eurodollar Deposits

Term:	Overnight to 5 years
Registration:	In full
Form:	Interest bearing
Multiples:	Any amount, but rate less attractive on amounts below $100,000
Settlement:	Normally 2 days forward in New York in Clearing House Funds
Interest accrues:	On 360-day basis
Interest paid:	At maturity
Tax:	No withholding taxes levied
Liquidity:	Non-redeemable and non-negotiable prior to maturity. Prearranged call features at penalty rates may occasionally be negotiated.
Rate:	Fixed, on the basis of the then prevailing inter-bank rates which are established daily in London. Different banks have different demands for money on a given day so their rates may not necessarily be at the inter-bank rate.

London Dollar Negotiable Certificates of Deposit (CDs)

These are the same as fixed-term Eurodollar deposits except that the investor receives a negotiable certificate which he can sell, at any time, through a member of the International CD Market Association whose trading activities are centered in London with links throughout North America and Europe. The rate on a CD does not normally differ significantly from the prevailing inter-bank rate. Other characteristics include:

Maturity:	New short-term CDs are normally issued in exact maturities of 1 to 12 months although most banks will create CDs for specific maturities.
	Broken date CDs are also available through a secondary market dealer.
Denominations:	Short-term CDs are issued in $1,000 multiples with a minimum of $25,000, while medium-term CDs (1-5 years) are available in a minimum of $10,000.
Form:	CDs are normally issued at full face value at a stated rate of interest.
	All calculations are based on a 360-day year and interest is paid on maturity, except in the case of CDs over 1 year in term where interest is annual.
Issuers:	A wide range of American, Canadian and European banks through their London branches.
Taxation and Legality:	No withholding or other taxes are imposed by U.K. authorities.
	London Dollar CDs are subject to U.K. exchange control regulations and the guidelines on foreign investment of the U.S. and Canadian authorities.
	They are construed under U.K. law. Sections 6 and 7 of Appendix G illustrates sample calculations for typical transactions.

Eurocommercial Paper

The growth and maturity of the Eurodollar market are reflected in its expanding range of financing techniques. One of these is Eurocommercial Paper (ECP). ECP is similar to commercial paper in the sense that it is an unconditional, unsecured promise by a non-bank issuer to repay a fixed sum on a fixed date upon presentation of the note at a stated place. The important distinction lies in certain legal characteristics which are necessary to make the paper salable in the Eurocurrency market, such as the applicability of U.S. Interest Equalization Tax and the inapplicability of withholding tax, since investors in the Eurocurrency market will generally not buy securities unless they are free of withholding tax.

Another important distinction is in the form of note used for ECP. The fact that the paper is sold across so many borders necessitates a special legal form in order that it can be used by an issuer from any country without modification. The most widely used type presently in circulation conforms to the requirements of the Geneva Code of 1930 and those of the U.K. Bills of Exchange Act, 1882, which in general provide that the jurisdiction where the note is issued governs its form, that the place of payment governs questions of payment, and that the place of endorsement governs questions of endorsement. By contrast, Canadian and U.S. paper is issued in conformity with the laws of a single jurisdiction and all questions are decided by its laws.

In the same way that commercial paper fits into the domestic money markets in Canada and the U.S., ECP fits into the Eurocurrency market, that is into the gap between yields on alternative short-term borrowings. In the Euromarket, London Dollar CDs and fixed deposits are the alternatives on the investment side, and their yield is the bid side of the

London inter-bank rate. The comparable borrowing cost at which a company can borrow for the relevant maturity is the spread over LIBOR. This gap in domestic markets is fairly wide (2 to 3% usually) due to regulations and structural factors, whereas in the unregulated Euromarket it is no more than ¾%, sometimes much less for first class credits.

For the borrower, the same advantages inherent in domestic commercial paper apply to ECP, perhaps with somewhat different weighting. It is an additional source of funds and perhaps taps money which is not being invested otherwise in the Eurocurrency market; it offers a cost-saving advantage over bank borrowing; and it strengthens the corporate name by spreading it among a wide circle of international lenders.

In general ECP, in the form of unsecured promissory notes issued by first class corporations, offers short-term investors a higher return than CDs of a similar term. Other characteristics include:

Maturity:	Varying periods under one year
Minimum Denomination:	Normally $50,000
Form:	ECP is usually issued at a discount from face value.
	All calculations are based on a 360-day year.
Taxation:	Withholding taxes are not normally applicable.
Negotiability:	Fully negotiable through a secondary market in London.

Chapter V

Borrowing in the Canadian Money Market

The previous chapters in this book serve to point out that the Canadian Money Market provides funds to all segments of Canadian government and business. Corporate commercial paper may be issued to augment working capital as an additional source of short-term funds; to allow for seasonal variations in cash flow; to finance expenditures that enjoy a rapid cash pay-back; or in anticipation of a long-term securities issue. Short-term paper also serves to familiarize financial markets with the credit of a particular issuer. At the same time, borrowing in the Money Market is generally a less expensive source of funds than alternative accommodation.

A Canadian corporation may raise funds in the Money Market either through issuing bankers' acceptances or commercial paper.

Bankers Acceptances

As outlined in Chapter III, this money market instrument is essentially a commercial draft drawn by a borrower for payment on a specified date and accepted, or guaranteed, by his bank. The bank's acceptance is signified by counter-signatures on the draft.

Once a draft of this type has been so countersigned, it becomes a Banker's Acceptance backed by the credit of the accepting bank. Acceptances are eligible for rediscount at the Bank of Canada, and as security for Day Money Loans with the chartered banks. Most Bankers' Acceptances are issued for a period not exceeding 90 days from date of acceptance.

The chartered banks have agreed to create acceptances in the following denominations: $100,000; $200,000; $300,-000; $500,000; $1,000,000; or any multiple thereof.

Use of Bankers' Acceptances

Generally any corporation can issue a Banker's Acceptance provided that the corporation's credit is deemed satisfactory for the purpose by its bank, and that the proceeds are to be used for purposes covered by the following statement which forms an integral part of the draft.

> "The drawer hereby certifies this draft is drawn in connection with such production or marketing of wares as is mentioned in section 18 (1) f of the Bank of Canada Act."

The section referred to reads as follows.

> "The Bank (of Canada) may,
> (f) buy and sell bills of exchange and promissory notes endorsed by a chartered bank drawn or issued in connection with the production or marketing of goods, wares and merchandise as defined in the Bank Act . . . and having a maturity not exceeding 90 days, excluding days of grace, from the date of acquisition by the Bank;"

Provided the proceeds are used for approved purposes, the chartered bank may agree to "accept" the commercial draft.

The borrower will also need to negotiate the stamping fee for this guarantee. Bank acceptance or stamping fees range from ½ to 1¼% per annum. In periods of monetary restraint, these fees tend to be lowered by the banks in an effort to encourage customers to seek financing in the open market. Conversely, in periods of monetary ease, these fees tend to increase as banks encourage open market borrowers to return as loan customers.

Raising Money

The borrower contacts a money market dealer and is quoted an annual rate of discount at which the dealer is prepared to purchase the draft once it has been accepted by the chartered bank. The rate is quoted on a present value basis and the price is calculated by the same formula as is used for Government of Canada treasury bills (see Section 1, of Appendix G). To this rate the borrower must add the stamping fee charged by his bank; then, if the borrower decides to proceed, the following steps are taken.

1. A draft is drawn for 90 days or less (provided the maturity falls on a banking day) on the special form provided for this purpose by the bank manager.

2. To render the Acceptance "negotiable" for market purposes, a corporate officer signs the face of the draft and endorses it in blank on the reverse.

3. The borrower obtains the bank's acceptance, which is signified by two official signatures on the draft itself.

4. The borrower then arranges for the money market dealer to take delivery of the Banker's Acceptance against payment of the discounted sum involved.

Handling at Maturity

All Bankers' Acceptances, wherever issued, are payable at maturity at the main offices of the accepting bank in both Toronto and Montreal. Arrangements can be made for pay-off in other centres.

The holder of the Bankers' Acceptance will present the draft, or will arrange to have the note presented on his behalf by an investment dealer, at the main branch in Toronto or Montreal of the bank concerned. The bank will then pay the holder and will, at the same time, arrange to charge the borrower's account in the branch at which the acceptance was created. Should there be a continuing requirement for money, a new acceptance can be arranged for settlement on the maturity date of the existing note.

Taxation Note

A corporation can charge as a pre-tax expense both the basic discount, within limits prescribed by the Income Tax Act, and the bank stamping fee.

Commercial Paper

Commercial paper is the name given to unsecured promissory notes issued by a corporation. These notes are backed by the general credit of the issuing corporation, by unused bank lines of credit, or by the guarantee of a parent corporation. Purchasers of commercial paper require appropriate documentation in support of their investment. While the nature of incorporation and type of paper may vary, the following corporate documents normally are made available. This documentation parallels the minimum requirements of Section 103 VI of the Rules and Regulations of the Investment Dealers Association of Canada.

(a) the latest annual report, preferably including a five-year comparative financial summary;

(b) a summary setting forth:
  (i) a brief résumé of the nature of the company and its operations;
  (ii) a statement regarding the purpose of the issue;
  (iii) a statement concerning the company's bank lines; and
  (iv) reference to the denominations in which notes may be issued;

(c) a copy of the borrowing by-law;

(d) a resolution of the company concerning borrowing of short-term funds;

(e) specimen signatures of corporate signing officers and a company certificate attesting to their validity;

(f) specimen short-term notes;

(g) a legal opinion by the company's counsel concerning the valid incorporation of the company, the issuance of notes, provincial jurisdictions in which the notes may be sold and the eligibility of the notes for investment under various federal and provincial statutes governing the investing powers of financial institutions such as life insurance companies and trust companies;

(h) in the event of a parent guarantee, parallel documentation pertaining to the parent is required.

Eligibility of Notes for Investment

The extent of eligibility of notes for investment by financial institutions is vital to the marketing process. Many of the major financial institutional lenders are restricted as to the securities in which they may invest by a number of federal and provincial statutes. Examples of some of the more significant acts and the financial institutions affected by these acts include:

(i) the Canadian and British Insurance Companies Act (Canada)—companies registered under Part III of this Act;

(ii) The Loan and Trust Corporations Act (Ontario) —a trust company or a loan corporation registered under this Act;

(iii) the Insurance Act (Ontario)—a joint stock insurance company, a fraternal society, a mutual insurance corporation and a cash-mutual insurance corporation, incorporated or organized under the laws of Ontario and governed by this Act;

(iv) the Trust Companies Act (Canada)—a trust company governed by this Act.

Of the restrictions and requirements contained in the above acts, two are of particular importance with respect to the eligibility of unsecured short-term notes for investment by various financial institutions. These are the dividend requirement and the interest coverage requirement which may be summarized as follows.

The notes will be eligible for investment by certain institutions if, with respect to the corporation issuing the notes:

(a) *dividend requirement*—that corporation has paid a dividend in each of the five years immediately preceding the date of investment at least equal to the specified annual rate upon all of its preferred shares or that corporation had paid or had earnings available for the payment of a dividend upon its fully paid common shares in each year for a period of five years that ended less than one year before the date of investment, provided that the dividends or the earnings available for dividends in each such year amounted to at least 4% of the average value at which the shares were carried in the capital stock account of the company during such years;

or

(b) *interest coverage requirement*—the earnings of that corporation in a period of five years ending less than one year before the date of investment have been equal in sum total to at least ten times and in each of any four of the five years have been equal to at least one and one-half times the annual interest requirements at the date of investment on all indebtedness of or guaranteed by it other than indebtedness classified as a current liability; if that corporation has a subsidiary, the earnings of the company and the subsidiary during the period of five years may be consolidated with due allowance for minority interests, provided that the indebtedness also be consolidated for the five-year period.

With respect to a corporation meeting the dividend requirement above:

—notes issued by or guaranteed by the corporation, wherever incorporated, are eligible for investment under The Loan and Trust Corporations Act (Ontario) and the Insurance Act (Ontario);

—notes issued by the corporation, wherever incorporated, are eligible for investment under the Canadian and British Insurance Companies Act (Canada); and

—notes issued by the corporation, if incorporated in Canada, are eligible for investment under the Trust Companies Act (Canada).

With respect to corporations meeting the interest coverage requirement above:

—notes issued by or guaranteed by the corporation, wherever incorporated, are eligible for investment under The Loan and Trust Corporations Act (Ontario), the Insurance Act (Ontario) and the Canadian and British Insurance Companies Act (Canada);

—notes issued by or guaranteed by the corporation, if incorporated in Canada, are eligible for investment under the Trust Companies Act (Canada).

General

The documents set forth above are normally presented in a brochure known as an *information memorandum* which is then widely disseminated to prospective lenders. In addition, there is usually an *agency agreement* between the borrower and dealer who is offering the company's notes. If a selling group of a number of dealers is formed, then a *selling group agreement* is made between the dealer acting as manager of the selling group and the balance of the dealers in the group. These agreements formalize the positions of the respective parties. An *operating procedure* will also have been devised prior to the sale of the first note which describes in detail the setting of rate structures, the arranging, issuance, delivery and redemption of the notes.

The borrowing strategy will be decided in consultation between the company concerned and Wood Gundy Limited, in light of the borrower's requirements and prevailing market conditions. These discussions are of a continuing nature, and comprise an integral part of our function as money market fiscal agents and advisors.

Mounting a commercial paper borrowing operation requires close liaison among the prospective borrower, his fiscal agent, and his legal counsel. Provided the borrower is credit-worthy and intends to issue notes not less than $50,000 in denomination and for a term not exceeding 1 year, the notes are regarded as exempt securities under most provincial securities legislation in Canada. Thus, the time interval from initial borrowing concept to note issuance and receipt of funds can be extremely short, numbered in terms of weeks. Prospective borrowers are invited to receive a customized note presentation with full documentation from Wood Gundy Limited. Appendix I contains a partial list of those commercial paper borrowers for whom Wood Gundy Limited acts. Scanning this list will indicate the wide variety of corporations and industries which use the commercial paper market as a continuing source of funds.

Chapter VI

Conclusion

This little book is only the tip of the iceberg. When an outside observer witnesses a dealer's money market operation in action for the first time, he is struck with a sense of total hard-paced confusion. What he sees when he observes a trading desk is a communications relay point for cash flow decisions that are being made in each treasury office in almost every corporation, institution, and government which utilize this market. It is a market that has no centre. Even within one organization, there is no centre. For example, Wood Gundy Limited begins its money market operation in Europe each day and closes it down in Vancouver sixteen hours later. The locus of decision making moves with time zones.

It is hoped that the bone structure of the Canadian Money Market has been revealed. In a world of kaleidoscopic change, in order to fill in the flesh and blood of the market, direct involvement is required.

Finally, each week, Wood Gundy publishes a Money Market Letter which contains brief commentary on recent market developments as well as a comparative review of rate structures in Canada and abroad. A sample of this letter is contained in Appendix I. The letter is available upon request.

Appendices

CANADIAN MONEY MARKET
By Asset Category as at December 31, 1969-1972
($ 000,000)

		1972	1971	1970	1969
1.	Government of Canada:				
	—Treasury Bills	4,160	3,830	3,625	2,895
	—Other, less than 3 years	5,856	5,300	5,200	5,191
2.	Provincial and Municipal Notes	567	493	464	439
3.	Bankers' Acceptances	390	403	395	174
4.	Chartered Banks:				
	—Corporate Deposits	8,265	6,375	4,600	3,622
	—Swapped Deposits	270	758	1,771	1,592
5.	Trust and Mortgage Loan Companies (under 1 year)	1,180	1,063	994	1,087
6.	Sales Finance Companies (under 1 year)	1,585	1,276	1,304	1,453
7.	Commercial Paper	1,135	1,246	957	777
		23,408	20,744	19,310	17,230
	Rate of Growth	12.8%	7.4%	12.1%	—
	Official Money Market	10,406	9,533	9,220	8,260
	Private Money Market	13,002	11,211	10,090	8,970
		23,408	20,744	19,310	17,230

APPENDIX B

INCIDENCE OF CANADIAN WITHHOLDING TAX
FOR U.S. RESIDENTS

Type of Security	Date of Security	Denominated In	Incidence of Tax
1. Federal Government Securities	on or before Dec. 20/60	Cdn. $ or U.S. $	free
	between Dec. 21/60 and Apr. 15/66	Cdn. $ or U.S. $	15%
	after Apr. 15/66	Cdn. $ or U.S. $	free
2. Provincial Securities	on or before Dec. 20/60	Cdn. $ U.S. $	15% free
	between Dec. 21/60 and Apr. 15/66	Cdn. $ or U.S. $	15%
	after Apr. 15/66	Cdn. $ or U.S. $	free
3. Municipal Securities	on or before Dec. 20/60	Cdn. $ U.S. $	15% free
	between Dec. 21/60 and Apr. 15/66	Cdn. $ or U.S. $	15%
	after Apr. 15/66	Cdn. $ or U.S. $	free
4. Bankers' Acceptances	(maximum 90-day term)	Cdn. $ only	15%
5. Canadian Chartered Bank Deposits	—U.S. Source	U.S. $	free
	—Cdn. Source	U.S. $	free
6. Certificates of Deposit or Bearer Deposit Notes of the Canadian Chartered Banks		Cdn. $	15%

7. All Other Debt Instruments	on or before Dec. 20/60	Cdn. $	15%
		U.S. $	free
	between Dec. 21/60 and Apr. 15/66	Cdn. $ or U.S. $	15%
	after Apr. 15/66	Cdn. $ or U.S. $	15%

Note:

The Canada-U.S. Reciprocal Tax Convention currently provides that the withholding tax should not exceed 15%. The Canadian Income Tax Act requires that, effective in 1976, the Canadian rate of tax withheld be increased to 25%. It is anticipated that the Canada-U.S. Reciprocal Tax Convention will be re-negotiated before 1976 and the agreed rate of withholding tax in the treaty will be subject to review.

APPENDIX C

IAC LIMITED

The Company

IAC Limited operates a diversified financing business from more than 200 offices across Canada. Traditionally, the main source of receivables has been the purchase of time payment paper (wholesale and retail) from sales of durable goods, representing 60% of the $1.364 billion total receivables. However, since 1946 IAC and its subsidiaries have expanded their operations to provide capital loans, consumer loans, residential mortgages, life and casualty insurance, and leasing facilities. Its subsidiaries include, among others, Niagara Finance Company Limited, Merit Insurance Company, and the Sovereign Life Assurance Company of Canada.

Denominations: Subject to a minimum of $5,000.

Principal Amount: The principal outstanding is not limited as to specific amount.

Form of Notes: Interest bearing or discount. Registered or bearer, short-term notes.

Eligibility: As outlined and qualified in the opinion of Counsel, the notes are eligible as investment under:

   (i) Canadian and British Insurance Companies Act (Canada)
   (ii) The Loan and Trust Corporations Act (Ontario)
   (iii) Trust Companies Act (Canada)
   (iv) Foreign Insurance Companies Act (Canada)
   (v) Pension Benefits Standards Act (Canada)
   (vi) Pension Benefits Act (Ontario)

Capital   IAC LIMITED and Subsidiaries
Structure: as at December 31, 1972

	$ millions	% of total
Secured demand bank loans	26.5	2.3
Secured short-term notes	313.9	27.2
Current long-term debt	63.8	5.5
Total short-term debt	404.2	35.0
Secured medium-term notes	106.2	9.2
Secured long-term notes	351.0	30.4
Debentures	100.1	8.7
Subordinated debentures	12.5	1.1
Shareholders' equity	179.5	15.6
	1,153.5	100.0

Liquidity Data: as at December 31

	1972	1971	1970	1969	1968
Times interest earned	1.7	1.7	1.6	1.6	1.6
Asset coverage	1.18	1.18	1.17	1.16	1.16
$\dfrac{\text{Debt—cash}}{\text{Shareholders' equity}}$	5.27	5.10	5.41	5.69	5.63

	1973
$\dfrac{\text{Maturing receivables}}{\text{Maturing borrowings}}$	1.57

$ millions	As at May 16/73 (2)
Bank lines of credit (1)	328.2
Bank loans	9.6
Unused bank lines	318.6
Commercial paper o/s	301.9
$\dfrac{\text{Unused bank lines}}{\text{Commercial paper borrowings}}$	1.06

(2) These are the combined figures of IAC Limited and Niagara Finance Company Limited.

(1) In Canada, bank lines of credit are ordinarily subject to elimination or contraction at any time at the option of the banks concerned.

Balance Sheet: December 31
($ millions)

Assets	1972	1971	Liabilities	1972	1971
Cash	28.2	30.6	Secured bank loan	26.5	26.0
Receivables—			Secured short-term notes	313.9	248.9
Wholesale	215.3	177.1	Accounts payable & accruals	77.3	49.6
Retail	606.9	517.0	Other current liabilities	17.2	21.4
Consumer loans	173.5	159.1	Current long-term debt	63.8	89.7
Mortgages	94.1	76.0	Total current liabilities	498.7	435.6
Commercial	31.3	39.5	Secured medium- &		
Leasing	220.7	147.6	long-term notes	457.2	378.6
Others (net)	9.5	4.6	Debentures	112.7	107.7
Short-term			Other liabilities	188.1	150.1
investments	33.6	63.5	Shareholders'		
Other assets	23.1	17.9	equity	179.5	160.9
	1,436.2	1,232.9		1,436.2	1,232.9

Income Statements: for the year ended December 31
($ thousands)

	1972	1971	1970	1969	1968
Sales	147,635	138,502	143,244	136,327	122,510
Operating profits	41,763	38,414	34,270	31,733	29,952
Net income before extraordinary items	21,994	19,415	16,862	15,484	14,658
Net income after extraordinary items	21,994	19,415	16,862	15,484	14,936
Profit margin	14.90%	14.01%	11.77%	11.36%	11.96%
Return on equity	12.92%	12.47%	11.47%	10.99%	10.82%

Latest Interim: ($ thousands)

	3 months ending March 31, 1973	3 months ending March 31, 1972
Sales	39,124	34,280
Net income before extraordinary items	5,337	5,000
Net income after extraordinary items	5,337	5,000

The information contained herein has been obtained from material published or made available by the Company. We make no representation that it is complete, accurate or current. This memorandum is not and under no circumstances is it to be construed as an offering of any securities.

APPENDIX D

BALANCE SHEET, DECEMBER 31, 1972
WOOD GUNDY LIMITED
and its subsidiaries

SUMMARY OF CONSOLIDATED FINANCIAL POSITION
DECEMBER 31, 1972
(with comparative figures at December 31, 1971)

ASSETS

	1972	1971
Current assets:		
Cash	$ 4,253,130	$ 943,934
Securities owned at market value plus accrued interest thereon—		
Maturing within six months	477,237,739	358,707,995
Maturing from six months to one year	46,361,657	28,325,386
Other	50,682,248	25,446,815
	574,281,644	412,480,196
Due from brokers and dealers	18,763,247	22,971,593
Due from clients	75,163,821	98,778,803
Other accounts receivable	2,281,331	1,277,101
Total current assets	674,743,173	536,451,627
Furnishings and leasehold improvements at cost, less accumulated depreciation and amortization	1,937,744	1,702,599
Stock exchange seats, at cost, and sundry assets	1,028,175	741,300
	$677,709,092	$538,895,526

LIABILITIES AND CAPITAL IN THE BUSINESS

Current liabilities:

Call loans	$347,614,533	$267,159,223
Securities sold but not yet purchased at market value plus accrued interest thereon—		
Maturing within six months	4,962,250	8,520,290
Other	10,251,535	8,509,252
	15,213,785	17,029,542
Payable to brokers and dealers	18,725,161	15,587,127
Payable to clients	270,506,949	217,083,599
Income taxes and accounts payable	5,484,241	5,390,715
Total current liabilities	657,544,669	522,250,206
Capital in the business:		
Subordinated loans	3,000,000	1,000,000
Debentures subordinated by shareholders and shareholders' equity	17,164,423	15,645,320
	20,164,423	16,645,320
	$677,709,092	$538,895,526

SUMMARY OF CONSOLIDATED INCOME AND RETAINED EARNINGS FOR THE YEAR ENDED DECEMBER 31, 1972
(with comparative figures for the year ended December 31, 1971)

	1972	1971
Gross revenue from operations (including dividend and interest income: 1972—$15,094,493; 1971—$12,044,867)	$ 45,315,083	$ 38,550,795
Deduct:		
General and administrative expenses	21,883,887	19,224,866
Interest expense	14,997,698	11,296,491
Depreciation	301,836	305,684
	37,183,421	30,827,041
Income before taxes and extraordinary item	8,131,662	7,723,754
Income taxes	3,874,543	3,824,417
Income for the year before extraordinary item	4,257,119	3,899,337
Extraordinary gain		623,391
Net income for the year	4,257,119	4,522,728
Retained earnings, beginning of year	8,946,690	6,016,045
	13,203,809	10,538,773
Deduct cash and stock dividends paid	879,050	1,592,083
Retained earnings, end of year	$ 12,324,759	$ 8,946,690

AUDITORS' REPORT

Wood Gundy Limited:

As auditors of Wood Gundy Limited and its subsidiaries, we made our normal examination of the company's detailed consolidated financial statement as at December 31, 1972, and reported thereon without qualification to the shareholders on February 5, 1973.

In our opinion the above summaries of consolidated financial position and consolidated income and retained earnings fairly summarize the related information contained in the detailed consolidated financial statements upon which we have reported.

Toronto, Canada,
February 5, 1973.

Clarkson, Gordon & Co.
Chartered Accountants

APPENDIX E

THIS AGREEMENT made this   day of   ,
19   , BETWEEN
(hereinafter called the "Lender") and WOOD GUNDY LIMITED
(hereinafter called "Wood Gundy") WITNESSETH THAT:

1.   The Lender shall lend to Wood Gundy and Wood Gundy
shall borrow from the Lender such amounts as the Lender and
Wood Gundy may agree upon from time to time at such rates of
interest and on such terms as to repayment as may be mutually
agreed upon from time to time. Each such transaction hereunder is hereinafter referred to as a "Loan" and all such transactions hereunder are hereinafter referred to collectively as the
"Loans".

2.   Wood Gundy shall pledge as collateral security for the
payment of each Loan a specified security or specified securities
(hereinafter referred to as "Pledged Collateral") agreed upon
between the Lender and Wood Gundy at the time such Loan is
made. Wood Gundy agrees that all Pledged Collateral shall be
either payable to bearer or duly endorsed in blank for transfer
by the registered holders thereof.

3.   The Pledged Collateral for all Loans outstanding from
time to time shall be held in safekeeping, either in the vaults of
Wood Gundy's bankers or Wood Gundy's own vault. At any time
and from time to time during normal business hours Wood
Gundy shall permit any person authorized in writing by the
Lender to examine the Pledged Collateral so held in safekeeping.
Wood Gundy shall confirm the Pledged Collateral so held in
safekeeping to the Lender on request.

4.   With the consent of the Lender Wood Gundy may sub-
stitute one or more securities of comparable value acceptable to
the Lender for a security or securities forming part of the
Pledged Collateral and shall forthwith notify the Lender in
writing of each such substitution.

5.   The Pledged Collateral of each Loan is hereby assigned to the Lender as collateral security for the payment of the principal and interest of such Loan and in the event that Wood Gundy shall fail to make any payment of principal of such Loan or of interest thereon when the same becomes due and payable the Lender shall be entitled to immediate possession of the Pledged Collateral and all evidences thereof and may sell the same or any part thereof at public or private sale or otherwise realize upon the same for such price and on such terms and conditions as the Lender deems best, the whole without advertisement or notice to Wood Gundy. All income from such Pledged Collateral after possession of it is taken by the Lender and the proceeds thereof, after deduction of all expenses thereof which shall be borne by Wood Gundy, shall be applied on account of the unpaid principal of such Loan and Interest thereon and the surplus, if any, shall be paid to Wood Gundy. If the Lender shall be entitled to possession of any Pledged Collateral as herein provided Wood Gundy shall cause the same to be delivered to the Lender as and when directed in writing by the Lender.

6.   When a Loan and all interest payable thereon is paid in full by Wood Gundy all Pledged Collateral for such Loan shall be forthwith released to Wood Gundy and freed from any pledge hereunder.

7.   Wood Gundy shall at any time if requested in writing by the Lender deliver the Pledged Collateral for any Loan to a branch in the City of Toronto of a chartered bank designated by the Lender for safekeeping and in such event the Lender shall pay all charges of the said bank for the safekeeping of such Pledged Collateral.

8.   Wood Gundy covenants that it has insurance under Brokers Blanket Bonds, Standard Form No. 14, insuring the Pledged Collateral and other securities in the aggregate amount of $20,000,000 against loss through any dishonest or fraudulent acts of its employees and through theft, mysterious unexplainable disappearance, damage or destruction and Wood Gundy covenants to maintain such insurance in force while any Loans are outstanding.

IN WITNESS WHEREOF the parties hereto have executed this Agreement.

By: ....

....

WOOD GUNDY LIMITED

By: ....

....

APPENDIX F

MARGIN REGULATIONS OF
INVESTMENT DEALERS ASSOCIATION
OF CANADA

Security Category	Capital Requirement (% of market value)
A. *Official Collateral*	
Treasury Bills (—6 months)	1/10 of 1%
Bankers' Acceptances (all maturities)	1/10 of 1%
Canadas (—6 months)	1/10 of 1%
Canadas (6 months—1 year)	1/2%
Canadas (over 1 year—3 years)	1%
B. *Provincial Collateral*	
Within 16 days	1/4%
17—182 days	1/2%
183 days—1 year	3/4%
over 1 years—3 years	1 1/2%
C. *Municipal Collateral*	
Within 16 days	1/4%
17—32 days	1/2%
33—92 days	1%
93—182 days	2%
183—272 days	2 1/2%
273 days—1 year	3%
over 1 year	5%
D. *Bank Paper*	
Within 32 days	1/4%
33—92 days	1/2%
93—182 days	1%
183—272 days	1 1/2%
273 days—1 year	2%
over 1 year—3 years	5%
E. *Acceptable Notes*	
Within 16 days	1/4%
17—32 days	1/2%
33—92 days	1%
93—182 days	2%
183—272 days	2 1/2%
273 days—1 year	3%
over 1 year—3 years	5%
F. *Other Notes*	
Within 1 year	4%
over 1 year—3 years	5%

Source: Investment Dealers Association of Canada, *The Blue Book.*

APPENDIX G

SAMPLE TRANSACTIONS AND YIELD CALCULATIONS

1. *Treasury Bills and Bankers' Acceptances*

   Problem: Find the purchase price of a 91-day treasury bill that matures at par, to yield 5.00%.

   Formula: $\text{Price} = \dfrac{1.00}{1.00 + \dfrac{(\text{yield} \times \text{term})}{365}}$

   Calculation: $\text{Price} = \dfrac{1.00}{1.00 + \dfrac{(.05 \times 91)}{365}}$

   $= .98769$

   Note: Treasury bills trade to the nearest 3 decimal points in price and 2 decimal points in yield.

2. (a) *Interest Bearing Finance or Commercial Paper*, and
   (b) *Interest Bearing Dealer Loans*

   Problem: Find the accrued interest on an investment at par of $100,000 for 91 days at 5.00%

   Formula: $\text{Accrued interest} = \dfrac{\text{par amount} \times \text{yield} \times \text{term}}{365}$

   Calculation: $\text{Accrued interest} = \dfrac{100,000 \times .05 \times 91}{365}$

   $= \$1,246.58$

3. *Discounted Finance or Commercial Paper*

   Problem: Find the purchase price of a $100,000 par note sold at a discount to mature at par, for a term of 91 days, at a rate 5.00% discounted to yield 5.063.

Formula: Price = par amount − discount

$$\text{Discount} = \frac{\text{par amount} \times \text{rate} \times \text{term}}{365}$$

$$= \$1,246.58$$

Price = \$100,000 − \$1,246.58
$$= \$98,753.42$$

Note: The discount of \$1,246.58 in this example is exactly equal to the accrued interest in example 2 above. However, in this instance the return is on an investment of \$98,753.42 (as opposed to par), hence the "effective" or "discounted" yield is 5.063 (as opposed to 5%).

4. *Interest Bearing Equivalent*

   Problem: Find the accrued interest on an investment at par of \$100,000 for 91 days at the interest bearing equivalent of 5% discounted (or 5.063)

   Formula: $\text{Accrued interest} = \dfrac{\text{par amount} \times \text{yield} \times \text{term}}{365}$

   Calculation: $\text{Accrued interest} = \dfrac{100,000 \times .05063 \times 91}{365}$

   $$= \$1,262.28$$

5. *Problem:*   Find the yield to a U.S. investor on a fully hedged investment using a 5⅛% interest bearing note and a .0005 pickup in the foreign exchange market.

   Solution:

Par Amount	Security	Principal
\$1,000,000	XYZ Corporation Limited 5.125 interest bearing Short-Term Note Dated: August 1, 1972 Due: October 30, 1972 Term: 90 days Guaranteed by: XYZ Corporation Fully hedged yield: 5.25%	\$1,000,000

Delivery Instructions: Due Bill (Letter of Undertaking)

Funds Hedged Through: A Canadian chartered bank or U.S. bank

Settlement Date	*Canadian*	*Exchange Rates*	*U.S. Funds*
August 1, 1972	$1,000,000.00	1.0150	$1,015,000.00 (Fed Funds)

Maturity Date			
October 30, 1972	$1,012,636.99	1.0155	$1,026,407.93 (Fed Funds)
15% NRT	1,895.55		
	1,010,741.44		

Yield Construction:

Yield on paper for 90 days	5.125
Yield due to .0005 pickup on Foreign Exchange	.20
TOTAL	5.325
All-in yield converted to 360-day basis $\dfrac{360}{365} \times 5.325$	5.25

6. *Problem:*   Find the cost for a short-term London Dollar CD of $100,000 issued at $7\frac{9}{16}\%$ for 90 days and bought by a secondary dealer at $6\frac{5}{16}\%$ with 43 days to maturity:

Solution: Proceeds

$$= \text{Principal} \times \frac{36{,}000 + (\text{issue rate} \times \text{total life})}{36{,}000 + (\text{quoted yield} \times \text{remaining life})}$$

$$= 100{,}000 \times \frac{36{,}000 + (7\frac{9}{16} \times 90)}{36{,}000 + (6\frac{5}{16} \times 43)}$$

$$= 100{,}000 \times \frac{36{,}000 + 680.6250}{36{,}000 + 271.4375}$$

$$= \$101{,}128.13$$

Proof

= Wood Gundy pays	$101,128.13
Value at maturity	101,890.63
	$ 762.50

$$\frac{762.50 \times 360}{101{,}128.13 \times 43} = 6.3125\% \quad (\text{i.e. } 6\tfrac{5}{16}\%)$$

7. *Problem:* Find the cost of a $10,000 CD issued at 9½% on September 20, 1970 to mature September 20, 1973, sold for settlement on July 13, 1971 at 8¼% for the remaining term to maturity. For a medium-term CD, the net proceeds are calculated by the repeated discounting of the maturity proceeds plus the successive annual interest payments.

Solution: The first step is to calculate the actual interest received annually and then, secondly, to discount these amounts:

(1) Interest from Sept. 20, 1972—Sept. 20, 1973: $963.19
Interest from Sept. 20, 1971—Sept. 20, 1972: $965.83
Interest from Sept. 20, 1970—Sept. 20, 1971: $963.19

(2) Proceeds at maturity = $10,000 + $963.19 = $10,963.19

Discount for 3rd year (365 days) at 8¼% :

$$10{,}963.19 \div \left(1 + \frac{8¼ \times 365}{100 \times 360}\right) = 10{,}117.00$$

Discount for 2nd year (366 days) at 8¼% :

$$(10{,}117.00 + 965.83) \div \left(1 + \frac{8¼ \times 366}{100 \times 360}\right) = 10{,}225.24$$

Discount for 69 days of 1st year at 8¼% :

$$(10{,}225.24 + 963.19) \div \left(1 + \frac{8¼ \times 69}{100 \times 360}\right) = 11{,}014.29$$

Proceeds are $11,014.29

APPENDIX H

CANADIAN EXEMPTION FROM UNITED STATES
BALANCE OF PAYMENTS MEASURES

The following exchange of letters between the Honourable Mitchell Sharp, Minister of Finance for Canada, and the Honourable Henry Fowler, Secretary of the Treasury of the United States was made public on March 7, 1968. These letters outline Canada's exemption from United States balance of payments measures. Subsequent documentation confirms and expands upon Canada's exemption. On February 13, 1973, George P. Schultz, Secretary of the Treasury, announced the intention of the United States Government to terminate the U.S. balance of payments measures at the latest by December 31, 1974.

Letter from Mr. Fowler to Mr. Sharp

Dear Minister Sharp:

Unique financial relations between our two countries have been a mutual support to both and to the international monetary system. These relations have served the interests of both our countries without interfering with the domestic policies of either.

As was said some years ago when it was agreed that Canada should be exempt under the interest equalization tax: "For many years the capital markets of the two countries have been closely interconnected and United States exports of capital to Canada have financed a substantial portion of the current account deficit with the United States. This need continues."

At the same time this special financial interdependence was underscored by the undertaking of Canadian authorities that it would not be the desire or intention of Canada to increase her foreign exchange reserves through the proceeds of borrowings in the United States.

It was agreed that active consultations would continue to strengthen the close economic relations between the two countries and facilitate measures for making the maximum practicable contribution to economic expansion and the strength and stability of both countries.

In keeping with this practice we and our colleagues have had the benefit of regular consultations prior to and since the New Years day announcement by President Johnson of the deterioration in 1967 of the United States balance of payments and the special program designed to bring the United States balance of payments to or close to equilibrium.

We have reviewed the new situation and the new program particularly because of some concern in financial markets over the potential effects of the program on Canada's financial position.

Our over-all financial arrangements have worked well and to our mutual advantage. Our special relationships in the financial field include:

All commercial bank lending to Canada regardless of maturities is exempt from the IET. Such loans to Canadian borrowers have priority under the federal reserve guidelines.

There are no restrictions on the amount of long term loans to Canadian borrowers which can be made by United States non-bank financial institutions. Such long term loans are exempt from the IET, from the direct investment program and from the federal reserve guidelines.

Canadian subsidiaries of United States companies as well as all other Canadian companies can come to the United States capital market and borrow free of the interest equalization tax to finance their investments in Canada.

We agree that the time has now come to adapt these special relations in the financial field to our mutual advantage in handling the new United States direct investment and federal reserve programs as well as Canada's reserve management policies.

The cardinal element in the present financial relationships between the United States and Canada is the fact that to the extent capital outflows from the United Sates to Canada of a kind now covered by the United States balance of payments measures are insufficient to finance Canada's current account deficit, Canadian borrowers would exercise their existing rights to borrow more in United States capital markets. Therefore any decline in the level of particular capital outflows to Canada from the level of past years caused by new United States measures could be expected to lead to increased borrowings by Canadian entities in the United States capital market.

In the light of this situation and to make sure that the flow of funds from the United States to Canada is adequate, the United States will undertake to exempt Canada from all the United States balance of payments measures affecting capital flows that are administered by the Department of Commerce or the Federal Reserve System.

By these arrangements Canada's financial position is assured insofar as capital imports from the United States are concerned, and the United States balance of payments objectives and program as announced on January 1st would not be affected.

I am sure that you will agree that it is desirable that we should continue to keep the economic and financial relationships between the two countries and with the rest of the world under continuing review, and that we should examine the detailed operation of this agreement and its impact on the balance of payments of both countries in the joint Canada-United States Ministerial Economic Committee and through regular meetings of our officials.

I am satisfied that these arrangements will provide mutual support to our payments position and hence strengthen the international monetary system.

Sincerely yours,

Henry H. Fowler

Letter from Mr. Sharp to Mr. Fowler

Dear Secretary Fowler:

I acknowledge receipt of your letter of today.

Canada has, as you are aware, a great interest in the strength and stability of the United States dollar and we have been deeply impressed by the steps you announced at the beginning of the year to reduce your balance of payments deficit. We have also been conscious of your desire to operate your program in a way which recognizes the special position of Canada.

I am of course very pleased that you have now reached the conclusion that you can, consistently with the objectives of your program, give further recognition to this special position by exempting Canada completely from your balance of payments program.

The unique position of Canada was reflected in the Interest Equalization Tax exemption and reserve target agreement reached in 1963. The Canadian government feels that the further steps you are now taking should be matched by further steps on the Canadian side. First to ensure that your balance of payments position is in no way impaired as a result of your action, I am informing you that it is our intention to take any steps necessary to ensure that the exemption from your program does not result in Canada's being used as a "pass-through" by which the purpose of your balance of payments program is frustrated.

It is also our intention to invest our entire holdings (apart from necessary working balances) of United States dollars in United States Government securities which do not constitute a liquid claim on the United States, with of course effective safeguards to our position should our reserve level require.

I agree that these arrangements are in the interests of both countries and in the general interest and that they provide further evidence of the close and mutually beneficial relationships between us.

Yours sincerely,

Mitchell Sharp

*Statement by the Minister of Finance dated May 3, 1968,
announcing guidelines for the Chartered Banks*

The Honourable E. J. Benson, Minister of Finance and President of the Treasury Board, announced today that following discussions with the chartered banks which the Bank of Canada undertook pursuant to the exchange of letters of March 7, 1968 between the Secretary of the United States Treasury and the Minister of Finance, the chartered banks are now conducting their operations in foreign currencies in such a way as to accord with the understandings reached in that exchange.

It will be recalled that Canada was granted exemption from the U.S. balance of payments measures affecting capital flows which are administered by the Department of Commerce and the Federal Reserve Board, and that in his letter to Mr. Fowler Mr. Sharp said that Canada would ensure that this exemption would not result in Canada's being used as a "pass through" by which the purpose of the United States balance of payments program would be frustrated.

The understanding reached with the chartered banks is embodied in three guidelines, which are appended. They provide in effect that Canadian banks will not be a channel for outflows of funds from the United States which impair the balance of payments of the United States without improving Canada's external position. The guidelines place no restrictions on the flow of funds from the United States to Canada through Canadian banking channels.

The Minister expressed his appreciation to the chartered banks for their co-operation.

1. The total of a bank's foreign currency claims on residents of countries other than Canada and the United States should not rise above the level of the end of February 1968 unless the increase is accompanied by an equal increase in its total foreign currency liabilities to residents of countries other than Canada and the United States.

2. If there should be a decline in the total of a bank's foreign currency liabilities to residents of countries other than Canada and the United States from the level at the end of February 1968 the bank should achieve an equal reduction in its total foreign currency claims on residents of countries other than Canada and the United States as quickly as the liquidity of such assets will permit.

3. Each bank should allow an increase in its U.S. dollar liabilities to residents of the United States from the level at the end of February 1968 only to the extent that the increase is fully matched by the sum of (1) the increase from that date in the bank's U.S. dollar claims on residents of Canada, (2) the decrease from that date in the bank's U.S. dollar liabilities to residents of Canada, and (3) the decrease from that date in the bank's own spot position in U.S. dollars.

Statement by the Minister of Finance dated July 24, 1968, announcing guidelines for Financial Institutions other than banks

The Honourable E. J. Benson, Minister of Finance, today recalled that in an exchange of letters on March 7, 1968, between the Secretary of the United States Treasury and the Minister of Finance, Canada was granted exemption from the U.S. balance of payments measures affecting capital flows which are administered by the Department of Commerce or the Federal Reserve Board, and that Canada undertook to ensure that this exemption would not result in Canada being used as a "pass-through" by which the purpose of the United States balance of payments program would be frustrated.

Mr. Benson noted that on May 3, 1968, the chartered banks had accepted a guideline which was designed to keep the total of each bank's foreign currency claims on residents of countries other than the U.S. and Canada from rising above the level of the end of February, 1968, unless the increase is accompanied by an equal increase in its total foreign currency liabilities to residents of countries other than Canada and the U.S.

Today he asked that a similar guideline be accepted by all other financial institutions operating in Canada, including trust companies, mortgage loan companies, sales finance companies, mutual funds, pension funds, insurance companies, investment companies, investment dealers, and small loan companies. The Minister asked that each of these financial institutions manage its affairs in such a way that the total of its foreign currency claims on residents of countries other than Canada and the United States, in the form of deposits, loans and portfolio investments in bonds and stocks, does not rise above the present level unless the increase is accompanied by an equal increase in its total foreign currency liabilities to residents of countries other than Canada and the United States, or arises from net earnings of foreign branches or subsidiaries.

The Minister said that his officials will be getting in touch with Canadian financial institutions either directly or through their associations to ask them to improve the information available to him on their foreign currency assets and liabilities.

In addition, Mr. Benson requested all Canadian investors to continue to comply with the request made in March, 1966 by the then Minister of Finance, the Honourable Mitchell Sharp, to all

Canadian investors, including all financial institutions, not to acquire securities denominated in Canadian or United States dollars which are issued by United States corporations or their non-Canadian subsidiaries and which are subject to the United States interest equalization tax if purchased by United States residents. Investments in such securities made by Canadian financial institutions in order to cover foreign currency liabilities to non-residents of Canada and the United States were exempt from this request. All Canadian financial intermediaries are asked not to facilitate transactions which would be contrary to this guideline concerning such "offshore" securities.

The Minister expressed confidence that Canadians would cooperate in protecting the national interest by following these guidelines. If there are cases in which financial institutions find that the conduct of their operations in accordance with these guidelines gives rise to special difficulties he asked that the institutions take these up with his officials. In particular he would be prepared to consider approval of investments in countries outside Canada and the United States to meet essential legal or customary requirements for cover for foreign currency liabilities in such countries, if this cover cannot otherwise be provided.

Statement by the Minister of Trade and Commerce dated September 19, 1968, announcing guidelines for Canadian Incorporated Companies, other than Financial Institutions

The Honourable Jean-Luc Pepin, Minister of Trade and Commerce, today announced a program applicable to Canadian incorporated companies, other than financial institutions, which is designed to ensure that their investments outside of Canada and the United States will be compatible with Canada's unrestricted access to the United States capital market.

This action is being taken as a follow-up to the arrangements set out in the exchange of letters between the United States Secretary of the Treasury and the Canadian Minister of Finance, dated March 7th, 1968, providing for the exemption of Canada from the United States balance of payments measures affecting capital flows. As part of the arrangement Canada undertook to ensure that the exemption did not result in Canada being used as a "pass-through", by which the purposes of the United States program are frustrated. Guidelines to implement this undertaking with respect to operations of the chartered banks were announced by the Minister of Finance in May and guidelines for other financial institutions were announced in July.

The Minister emphasized that it is important that the flow of investment overseas should not be increased as a consequence of the unrestricted access of Canadian business to the United States capital market. In this connection the Minister noted that annual investment overseas by Canadian non-financial companies was normally modest in amount, and a continuation of a normal volume of Canadian investment of this kind would be in order. The Government is not proposing the establishment of quotas for individual non-financial companies in order to ensure that the aggregate flow of investment overseas from such companies is held to moderate dimensions but the Government is instead requesting that these companies adhere to certain priorities as indicated in the following guidelines:

> As regards investment in continental Western Europe, Canadian companies are asked not to embark on new investment programs or otherwise increase their assets in such countries in any way involving the transfer of capital funds or other forms of financing from Canada or the United States except in cases where firm commitments have been made or where it can be clearly demonstrated that such investment could be expected to bring unusually large and early benefits to Canada's trade and payments position and cannot be adequately financed from overseas sources.

> As regards investment in other developed countries overseas, companies are asked to exercise restraint in embarking on new investment undertakings which involve capital transfers or other forms of financing from Canada or the

United States and to give priority to investment which will contribute importantly to improvement in Canada's trade and payments.

The general restraint to be exercised with respect to capital transfers to overseas countries is not intended to inhibit desirable investment in less developed countries.

Nothing in these guidelines is to restrict the financing of Canadian exports.

As part of the program Canadian incorporated companies are being asked to provide information quarterly on international capital transfers actually made, and also to provide information on planned capital transfers to overseas countries for 1968 and 1969 in cases where transfers in excess of $200,000 annually are contemplated. The forward plans submitted will be carefully reviewed in light of the need to keep total Canadian investment overseas within moderate dimensions consistent with the exemption from the United States balance of payments restrictions. Particular attention will be given to programs which involve the use of funds obtained from the United States either directly or indirectly.

Statement by the Honourable Mitchell Sharp, Minister of Finance, to the House of Commons, March 16, 1966.

When the United States balance of payments guidelines were being discussed in this house on February 2, I said that it would be most undesirable if the effect of these guidelines was to induce strong new demands upon capital markets in Canada. I also indicated that if necessary we would take whatever action is appropriate to protect Canadian interests. Prior to our meeting with the United States Secretaries in Washington it seemed clear that pressures on our capital markets were being accentuated as an indirect result of the United States guidelines, and we discussed this with them.

Under the guidelines, United States companies are being encouraged to raise funds abroad for their international operations. In response to this, well known United States companies and their foreign subsidiaries are issuing dollar securities for sale outside the United States. To the extent that this search for funds abroad by United States companies attracts funds from Canada, it puts abnormal pressure on the Canadian market and could force Canadian borrowers to rely more heavily on the United States capital market.

It has been, and continues to be, the policy of the government to encourage Canadians to invest their savings in Canadian development. We are now entering our sixth consecutive year of significant economic growth. Heavy demands are being made on our capital markets as Canadian industry expands its capacity and improves its efficiency and as Canadian governments and municipalities undertake to provide the many services required by our expanding economy.

To meet this situation I am, on behalf of the government, making the following request today to Canadian investors.

To help ensure that Canadian savings are available to meet the present large demands for capital in Canada the government is asking all Canadian investors, including financial institutions such as the banks, life insurance companies, and trust and loan companies, as well as other corporations, pension funds and individuals, not to acquire securities, denominated in Canadian or United States dollars, which are issued by United States corporations or their non-Canadian subsidiaries and which are subject to the United States interest equalization tax if purchased by United States residents. Investments in such securities made by Canadian financial institutions and pension funds to cover foreign currency liabilities to non-residents of Canada and the United States are exempt from this request.

Canadian borrowers have co-operated with the government's requests in the past for the exercise of some temporary restraint in borrowing abroad in the national interest. I feel certain that Canadian investors on their side will co-operate fully with this request which is also in the national interest.

For some time the Bank of Canada and the Department of Finance have, in answer to enquiries, been discouraging the issue of securities in Canada by foreign borrowers. I feel that we should continue to discourage such issues since the use of Canadian savings in this way could bring increased pressures on our capital market and lead to increased borrowings in the United States by Canadians under the exemption from the interest equalization tax. I am confident that our financial institutions will continue to assist us in carrying out this policy.

FINANCE RELEASE FROM INFORMATION SERVICES OTTAWA

For release: Immediate   Ottawa, May 25, 1972
                                          72-60

Guidelines on Capital Outflow

Finance Minister John N. Turner today announced amendments to the guidelines relating to capital outflow, instituted in 1966 and 1968.

The first guideline, introduced in March, 1966, requested all Canadian investors, individuals and corporations, not to acquire "off-shore" securities issued by U.S. companies and their foreign subsidiaries for sale outside the United States. At the same time it was announced that the Bank of Canada and the Department of Finance had for some time been discouraging the issue of securities in Canada by foreign borrowers.

In March, 1968, Canada was granted an exemption from the U.S. balance of payments measures introduced at the beginning of that year. Both banks and non-bank financial institutions were asked not to increase their foreign currency claims on residents of countries other than Canada or the United States unless such an increase was accompanied by an equal increase in the total foreign currency liabilities to such countries, or arose from net earnings of foreign branches or subsidiaries. In March, 1971, the bank and the non-bank financial institutions were informed that transfers of Canadian dollars to residents of third countries should be regarded in the same way as transfers of other currencies.

These requests were made to ensure that Canada's exemption from the United States interest equalization tax and the United States balance of payments measures affecting capital flows would not lead to Canada becoming a "pass-through" by which the purpose of the U.S. balance of payments program might be frustrated.

The changes in the guidelines announced today by the Minister of Finance are of a limited nature and are designed to bring the Canadian program more closely into line with the U.S. program.

The changes are as follows:

1. Securities denominated in Canadian dollars issued or guaranteed by central governments or central banks of developing countries are exempted from the request in the 1966 guideline.

2. Canadian dollar term loans by banks and other financial institutions made to or guaranteed by central governments or central banks of developing countries are exempted from the 1968 guidelines.

3. All new export financing, designed to facilitate Canadian exports, by banks and other financial institutions, is exempted from the 1968 guidelines.

These changes take effect retroactive to March 31, 1972. The Minister expressed his appreciation to all Canadian investors for their co-operation concerning the guidelines program and asked for their continued support.

APPENDIX I

Sample of weekly letter published by Wood Gundy

The Money Market

April 12, 1973

The Canadian Bank Rate Change

From a technical point of view, Bank Rate in Canada is that rate charged by the Bank of Canada on initial advances made by the central bank to the chartered banks. Such advances are made whilst the central bank is performing its classical lender of last resort function. Bank Rate has also come to be identified as an indicator of the direction of domestic monetary policy. In addition, Bank Rate is often identified with an international monetary policy objective. When the domestic policy intent is inconsistent with the international policy intent, the Bank of Canada has, upon occasion, taken the trouble of explaining which is intended. The increase in Bank Rate from 4¾% to 5¼% last Friday evening, for effect Monday, April 9, is such an occasion.

The Governor of the Bank of Canada clearly indicated that, from a domestic point of view, ". . . monetary policy in Canada will continue to be expansionary . . .". From an international policy point of view, the relative effective yield gap between the United States and Canadian banking systems had apparently become too large. The cosmetics of the official explanation were that the previous yield gap was creating a too rapid growth rate in Canadian bank assets, presumably implying that international corporations were drawing down Canadian lines and employing the funds elsewhere.

The banking system responded immediately by raising prime rate ½% to 6½% and increasing the Winnipeg Agreement ceiling by ½% to 6% on CD's and BDN's having a term to maturity not exceeding one year. Commercial paper rates as well as trust company rates have generally adjusted by equivalent amounts. After initial gyrations, the forward market on the Canadian Dollar appears to have adjusted to roughly equilibrate the Southbound flows of funds into the London CD market by Guideline-exempt lenders and the Northbound flows of funds into the Canadian paper market by U.S. corporate lenders. As Peggy Lee would say ". . . is that all there is"—to a Bank Rate change? Whatever was going on before in the Canadian money market continues as before, but with a new set of markers.

There probably is no *a priori* answer to the question of an appropriate yield spread between administered prices, such as prime loan rates, other than trial and error. Presumably if, after a spell, the rate of increase in Canadian bank assets does not decelerate, or rather if the implied exodus on the part of international corporations does not abate, then Canada is in for further increases in Bank Rate. Only time will tell.

What is really intriguing is the timing of the Bank Rate change —just as the Canadian Dollar had dipped below par U.S. Do we now regard par with the U.S. Dollar as the floor for the Canadian Dollar? If market forces are not strong enough to keep the Dollar at par or higher, then can we rely on the Bank of Canada to take overt action to keep it above? The seeming open market trading by the Bank of Canada during the Michelin Tire run-down last fall and the current timing of the Bank Rate change are not inconsistent with this hypothesis.

Peter Campbell, Toronto

The Hedge Market

The Bank Rate change of last week led to a narrowing of the forward premium on the Canadian Dollar. Initially, the forward market appeared to overreact due to the uncertainty of where Canadian short-term rates would settle and, in particular, what changes the chartered banks would make both in their prime rate and rates paid on certificates of deposit. During this period of uncertainty, the premium on the forward sale of Canadian narrowed in the one month area from a $.0020 premium (235 basis points) on Friday, April 6, to a low of $.0014 (170 basis points) by mid-morning on Monday, April 9. Similar changes were recorded in the forward purchase of Canadian with these rates narrowing from $.0022 cost (259 basis points) to $.0017 (200 basis points). By Tuesday, when the Canadian interest rate uncertainty had been resolved, stability had returned as the forwards adjusted to reflect the narrower differential between U.S. and Canadian rates. There was a resumption both of the fully hedged flow of U.S. funds into Canada on a small scale and fully hedged funds into the Eurodollar CD market, but on a reduced scale because of the narrowing of absolute rates between Europe and Canada.

Paul Bull, Toronto

United States Market

The recent recovery in our short-term markets is viewed with some skepticism from this corner.

The turnaround was initiated by the Federal Reserve early in the statement week ending April 11th through outright purchases of treasury bills and repurchase agreements. The 3-month bills which were auctioned at 6.53% on April 2nd are now 6.17% bid. In addition, rates moved lower by perhaps .25% on a broad range of money market instruments.

We are, however, facing a period of heavy run-offs of CD's which were purchased for the April 15th tax date and rates on newly issued CD's are edging upward again. Rates appear poised to renew their upward course.

Charles Barrington Jr., New York

Eurocurrency Market

Liquidity conditions continued to improve this week as day-to-day Eurodollar rates moved down to a 7¼% level helped, of course, by an easier Fed Funds market. London banks have been bidding much less aggressively for money, many below the base in the fixed-date periods (i.e. 1-12 months) which, however, have been quoted lower only very reluctantly. As suggested here last week, New York money market rates are the predominant factor right now in the establishment of Eurodollar rates and, despite the present ease in New York and the likelihood of an even-keel Fed policy in the weeks ahead, conditions still point to higher money costs.

Along with this outlook, there is every indication that the Eurodollar market will become increasingly liquid. Exchange controls and the snake rule out major dollar shifts into European currencies, and currency positions and leads and lags are slowly unwinding. In addition, the Italian foreign exchange office this week offered to return to the Italian commercial banks part of the roughly $650 million in dollar swaps which have been rolled since December. These Dollars initially were borrowed in the Eurodollar market. It has been widely suggested that a run-back of Eurodollars into the U.S. would be useful, but it is unlikely that U.S. authorities would appreciate a reflow right now. The Fed has finally reined in money supply and any significant inflow of Eurodollars would undo these efforts.

Gary Shaw, London, England

EUROCURRENCY INTEREST RATES

	U.S. Dollars	D Marks	Swiss Francs	Dutch Guilder	Sterling
1 Month	7.75	3.50	2.9375	.50	10.00
3 Months	7.9375	3.50	3.25	1.50	10.125
6 Months	8.0625	3.50	4.3125	2.25	10.50
1 Year	8.125	4.00	5.125	3.625	10.625

THE FOREIGN EXCHANGE MARKET

	1 Month	2 Months	3 Months	6 Months	9 Months	1 Year
*Hedge Rates**						
Canada to U.S.	−2.10	−2.04	−1.88	−1.66	−1.36	−1.13
U.S. to Canada	+1.86	+1.92	+1.80	+1.62	+1.23	+1.03
Representative Short Term Paper Yields (Equivalent Credits)						
Canadian investing in Canada	5.375	5.50	5.625	5.875	6.125	6.50
Canadian investing in U.S. (Hedged)	4.775	4.835	5.12	5.59	5.89	—
American investing in U.S.	6.875	6.875	7.00	7.25	7.25	—
American investing in Canada (Hedged)	7.235	7.42	7.425	7.495	7.355	7.53
Canadian Bank—U.S. Dollar Deposits						
Canadian Residents	7.00	7.25	7.375	7.375	7.375	7.375
U.S. Residents	7.00	7.25	7.375	7.375	7.375	7.375
Third Country Residents (London U.S. $ C.D.)	7.75	7.75	7.75	8.00	8.00	8.00

*Rates in Annual Yield Terms   Pickup + Loss − Flat . . .

	FRI.	MON.	TUES.	WED.	THURS.
Spot Canadian in U.S. Funds	99.88	100.06	100.04	99.94	100.00
Spot £ Sterling in U.S. Funds	2.4815	2.4840	2.4845	2.4885	2.4880
Free Gold Price (London Afternoon Fixing)	90.75	91.00	91.00	91.25	90.90

SHORT AND MEDIUM TERM RATES

Commercial and Finance Co. Paper	Demand	1-15 days	16-29 days	30-59 days	60-89 days	90-119 days	120-179 days	180-269 days	270-365 days
High	5⅜	5⅜	5⅜	5½	5⅝	5¾	5⅞	6	6⅛
Low	5¼	5¼	5¼	5⅛	5¼	5⅜	5⅜	5½	5½

Provincial and Municipal Treasury Bills and Notes

	Demand	1-15 days	16-29 days	30-59 days	60-89 days	90-119 days	120-179 days	180-269 days	270-365 days
Alberta Municipal Financing Corp.	—	—	—	5.30	5.40	5.50	—	—	—
Manitoba	—	—	—	5.30	5.40	5.50	—	—	—
Montreal (City)	—	—	—	—	—	5.70	—	—	—
Ontario	—	—	—	5.30	5.40	5.50	—	—	—
Ontario Hydro	—	—	—	4.90	5.10	5.30	5.30	5.60	5.85
Quebec Hydro	—	—	—	4.50	4.75	4.85	4.85	5.00	5.25
Saskatchewan	—	—	—	5.30	5.40	5.50	—	—	—

Chartered Banks

	Demand	1-15 days	16-29 days	30-59 days	60-89 days	90-119 days	120-179 days	180-269 days	270-365 days
Cdn. Dollar Deposits	—	4.00	4.75	5.375	5.50	5.625	5.625	5.75	6.00
Cdn. Dollar "Swapped" Deposits	—	4.52	4.65	4.71	5.06	5.46	5.54	5.64	6.20

(continued)

Trust Companies	—	—	—	5.25	5.50	5.75	5.75	5.875	6.00

Bankers Acceptances

| Bid | — | — | — | 5.35 | 5.50 | 5.60 | — | — | — |
| Offered | — | 5.20 | 5.20 | 5.25 | 5.40 | 5.50 | — | — | — |

	1-1½ Years	1½-2 Years	2-2½ Years	2½-3 Years	3-4 Years	4-5 Years	5-6 Years
Chartered Banks	6½	6½	6¾	6¾	7	7¼	7⅜
Finance Companies	6	6	6½	6½	6⅞	7⅛	7⅜
Trust Companies	6¼	6¼	6¾	6¾	7	7	7½

GOVERNMENT OF CANADA BONDS TO 3 YEARS IN TERM

	Issue		Bid	Ask	Yield %
6½	1 July	1973	100.25	100.30	4.93
6¾	1 July	1973	100.30	100.35	4.93
5	1 Oct.	1973	99.75	99.85	5.32
5¼	1 Dec.	1973	99.75	99.85	5.48
6¼	1 Dec.	1973	100.40	100.50	5.41
5¾	1 Feb.	1974	100.00	100.10	5.61
5	1 Apr.	1974	99.35	99.45	5.60
7¼	1 Apr.	1974	101.50	101.75	5.35
7	15 June	1974	101.45	101.55	5.60
6	15 June	1974	100.30	100.40	5.63
8	1 Oct.	1974	104.00	104.50	4.76
4¼	1 Dec.	1974	97.20	97.30	6.01
5½	1 Dec.	1974	99.10	99.20	6.02
7¼	1 Apr.	1975	101.90	102.10	6.09
6½	1 Apr.	1975	100.50	100.70	6.11
7¼	1 July	1975	102.00	102.20	6.17
5½	1 Oct.	1975	98.10	98.20	6.29
7¼	15 Dec.	1975	102.25	102.75	6.12
5½	1 Apr.	1976	97.45	97.55	6.46

E.&O.E.   *This is not and under no circumstances is this memorandum to be construed as an offering of any securities.*

MONEY MARKET SUMMARY

	Today	Last Week	Last Month	Last Year
Bank Rates				
Canada	5¼	4¾	4¾	4¾
U.S. (N.Y. Fed.)	5½	5½	5½	4½
U.K.	8	8½	8¾	5
Prime Rates				
Canada	6½	6	6	6
U.S.	6½	6½	6¼	5
Treasury Bills				
(avg. tender) %				
Canada 3 month	4.73	4.48	3.99	3.70
6 month	5.11	4.81	4.30	4.02
U.S. 3 month	6.17	6.53	5.81	3.73
U.K. 3 month	7.45	7.88	8.22	4.31
Bankers' Acceptances				
Canada 3 month	5.55	5.05	4.95	5.65
U.S. 3 month	7.00	7.00	6.125	4.625
Chartered Bank Deposits				
CDN. Dollar 3 month	5.625	5.125	5.125	5.75
"Swapped" 3 month	5.46	5.28	4.67	5.26
Representative				
Short Term Paper				
Canada 3 month	5.625	5.25	5.125	6.00
U.S. 3 month	7.125	7.125	6.25	4.625
Forward Exchange Hedge Rates				
(Annual Yield Basis)				
Canada to U.S. 3 month	−1.88	−2.16	−1.88	+ .76
U.S. to Canada 3 month	+1.80	+2.08	+1.72	− .84
Yield Differential Can-U.S.				
Federal Government Bonds				
5 year	.18	.18	.11	.57
LONG TERM (Average)	1.32	1.27	1.13	1.21
Canadian Dollar				
In terms of U.S.†	100.02	100.02	100.80	100.35

† Former   (I.M.F. Parity Range 91.575 - 93.425
            (Operational Range 91.74 - 93.24

AMONG THE COMPANIES FOR WHOM WE ACT
IN THE PROMISSORY NOTE MARKET

Alberta Wheat Pool
The Algoma Steel Corporation, Limited
Avco Financial Services Canada Limited
BBC Mortgage Ltd.
BBC-RI Services Ltd.
B. C. Central Credit Union
Bell Canada
Beneficial Finance Co. of Canada
Benson & Hedges (Canada) Limited
BNS Mortgage Corporation
B P Oil Limited
British Columbia Forest Products Limited
British Columbia Packers Limited
Builders Financial Co. Limited
Canada Development Corporation
Canada Malting Co., Limited
Canada Packers Limited
Canadian Acceptance Corporation Limited
Canadian General Electric Company Limited
Canadian General Electric Credit Limited
Canadian Industries Limited
Canadian Ingersoll-Rand Company Limited
Canadian Pacific Securities Limited
Canadian Utilities, Limited
Canron Limited
Chemco Leasing Limited
Citicorp Financial Services Canada Ltd.
CMB Holdings Limited
Commercial Credit Corporation Limited
The Consumers' Gas Company
Co-operative Credit Society of Manitoba Limited
Crédit Foncier Franco-Canadien
John Deere Limited
Distillers Corporation Limited
Dominion Bridge Company, Limited
Dominion Foundries and Steel, Limited
Dominion Textile Limited
Dow Chemical of Canada, Limited
Du Pont of Canada Limited
The T. Eaton Acceptance Co. Limited
First Northamerica Investments Ltd.

FMC of Canada Limited
Ford Motor Credit Company of Canada, Limited
General Distributors of Canada Ltd.
General Foods, Limited
General Motors Acceptance Corporation of Canada, Limited
Genstar Limited
B. F. Goodrich Canada Limited
Gulf Minerals Canada Limited
Hudson's Bay Company
IAC Limited
Imasco Limited
IMB Leasing Limited
Imperial Oil Limited
International Harvester Credit Corporation of Canada Limited
The International Nickel Company of Canada, Limited
Kelly, Douglas & Company, Limited
Laurentide Financial Corporation Ltd.
Lever Brothers Limited
MacMillan Bloedel Limited
Manitoba Pool Elevators
Maple Leaf Mills Limited
MarMid Financial Services Limited
Massey-Ferguson Finance Company of Canada Limited
Motorola Canada Limited
National Agri-Services Limited
Niagara Finance Company Limited
Noranda Mines Limited
Northern and Central Gas Corporation Limited
The Ogilvie Flour Mills Company, Limited
Pacific Petroleums Ltd.
Petrofina Canada Ltd.
Philips Electronics Industries Ltd.
Pioneer Grain Company, Limited
Polysar Limited
Redpath Industries Limited
Robin Hood Multifoods Limited
The Royal Trust Company Mortgage Corporation
RoyMor Ltd.
RoyNat Ltd.
Saskatchewan Wheat Pool
Simpsons, Limited
Simpsons-Sears Limited
Sperry Rand Canada Limited
Sperry Rand Financial Corporation (Canada) Ltd.

Standard Brands Limited
Stauffer Chemical Company of Canada, Ltd.
The Steel Company of Canada, Limited
Steinberg's Limited
Texaco Canada Limited
Traders Group Limited
Transamerica Financial Corporation of Canada Ltd.
TransCanada PipeLines Limited
Union Acceptance Corporation Limited
Union Carbide Canada Limited
United Co-operatives of Ontario
United Dominions Corporation (Canada) Limited
United Grain Growers Limited
Volvo Canada Ltd.
Wardley Canada Ltd.
Weldwood of Canada Limited
George Weston Limited
Weyerhaeuser Canada Ltd.
Woodward Stores Limited

WOOD GUNDY LIMITED

MEMBER

Investment Dealers Association of Canada
The Toronto Stock Exchange
Montreal Stock Exchange
Canadian Stock Exchange
Vancouver Stock Exchange
Winnipeg Commodity Exchange
Euro-clear Clearance System Limited

DIRECTORS

C. L. Gundy* *Chairman*
J. N. Cole* *Vice Chairman*
C. E. Medland* *President & Chief Executive Officer*
Vice Presidents
P. J. Chadsey
J. R. LeMesurier*
J. N. Abell*
D. C. H. Stanley*
I. S. Steers*
R. E. Beale*
J. L. McAlpine* *Treasurer*
J. M. G. Scott*
R. T. Morgan
R. M. Hanbury
G. S. Swindell
J. A. Black
N. F. Elsey
R. D. Thompson
I. C. Woolley *Secretary*
P. A. T. Campbell
M. R. Graham
W. R. Whitbeck
C. A. C. Dobell

Member of Executive Committee

VICE-PRESIDENTS
W. J. Cathro
W. S. Dinnick
T. R. Gibson
J. A. G. Grant
P. D. Hearn
L. Kadak
C. R. Moses *Controller*
P. E. Newdick
W. Pepall
T. C. W. Reid
H. D. Ross
J. T. Spurgen
F. B. C. Tice

OTHER OFFICERS
M. M. Armstrong *Assistant Secretary*
K. F. Oxenham *Assistant Secretary*
R. D. Hawkins *Assistant Treasurer*
P. A. Upson *Assistant Treasurer*
J. D. Bates *Assistant Controller*
E. T. Carlson *Assistant Controller*
N. F. Sherwood *Assistant Controller*

ASSISTANT VICE PRESIDENTS
J. W. Beacham
W. D. Bean
R. T. Bixley
A. H. T. Crosbie
C. Crossman
J. R. Daly
C. J. Funston
H. M. Heath
J. R. Hutchinson
F. B. Jacob
R. M. Kerr
M. G. McKibbin
J. R. Richards
M. S. Richardson
W. L. Ridley   A. Smith
C. L. E. Seagram   B. P. Steel
G. A. Shaw   J. E. Thomson
K. L. Slater   C. J. Wakefield

WOOD GUNDY INCORPORATED

MEMBER

New York Stock Exchange
Midwest Stock Exchange
Philadelphia-Baltimore-Washington Exchange
National Association of Securities Dealers, Inc.

OFFICERS

G. E. King *President*
R. A. Berneburg *Vice President*
R. D. Brearley *Vice President*
C. M. Kaeppel *Vice President*
H. C. B. Lindh *Vice President & Treasurer*
C. R. Malcolm *Vice President*
R. S. Sinclair *Vice President*
P. F. Ricciardi *Secretary*

WOOD GUNDY (INTERNATIONAL) LIMITED

I. S. A. Fraser *Managing Director*

WOOD GUNDY OFFICES

WOOD GUNDY LIMITED

Head Office
Royal Trust Tower
P.O. Box 274, Toronto-Dominion Centre
Toronto, Ontario M5K 1J5
Telephone: (416) 362-4433

Montreal
Royal Bank Building
1 Place Ville Marie
Montreal 113, P.Q.
Telephone: (514) 878-4717

Winnipeg
280 Broadway Avenue
Winnipeg, Manitoba R3C 0R8
Telephone: (204) 942-6141

Vancouver
Pacific Centre
Box 10017
1700—700 West Georgia Street
Vancouver 2, B.C.
Telephone: (604) 683-8311

London, England
30 Finsbury Square
London EC2A 1SB
Telephone: 01-628-4030

Tokyo, Japan
Imperial Hotel, Suite 407
1-1, Uchisaiwai-cho, 1, chome
Chiyoda-ku, Tokyo 100
Telephone: 504-2040

Offices in:

Halifax	North Bay
Saint John	Oshawa
Quebec City	Ottawa
Barrie	Regina
Hamilton	Saskatoon
Kingston	Calgary
Kitchener	Edmonton
London, Ont.	Victoria

WOOD GUNDY INCORPORATED
New York
100 Wall Street
New York, N.Y. 10005
Telephone: (212) 344-0633

WOOD GUNDY (INTERNATIONAL) LIMITED
Toronto
Royal Trust Tower
P.O. Box 274, Toronto-Dominion Centre
Toronto, Ontario, Canada M5K 1J5
Telephone: (416) 362-4433

Index